WHAT YOU DON'T KNOW CAN COST YOU MONEY!

Discover . . .

- HOW TO GET *FREE* HELP FOR TRAVELING, PARENTING, CREDIT PROBLEMS, HEALTH PROBLEMS, ADOPTION, COLLEGE FINANCIAL AID, INSURANCE...AND MORE

- EASY RECIPES TO FEED A FAMILY ON LESS

- A QUICK WAY TO SHINE SILVER...GET YOUR CLOTHES DRY... COVER FURNITURE SCRATCHES...CLEAN THE COMMODE

- WHERE YOU CAN TRY OUT USED SMALL APPLIANCES...AND THEY'LL COST YOU NEXT TO NOTHING

- HOW TO UNFREEZE YOUR CAR LOCK WITHOUT CALLING A LOCKSMITH

- THE TWINS' PERSONAL FAVORITE RETAIL STORE, GROCERY STORE, AND CLOTHING STORE

- SAFE INSECTICIDES AND FERTILIZERS FROM COMMON HOUSEHOLD PRODUCTS

Plus the twins have included cutouts, poems and prayers to copy, checklists, a phone book, and other great freebies in . . .

LIVING ON A SHOESTRING

living
on a
SHOESTRING

the tightwad twins
Ann Fox Chodakowski
and Susan Fox Wood

A Dell Trade Paperback

A DELL TRADE PAPERBACK

Published by
Dell Publishing
a division of
Bantam Doubleday Dell Publishing Group, Inc.
1540 Broadway
New York, New York 10036

This book is a compilation of suggestions by the authors on saving money. Neither the publisher nor the authors takes any responsibility for any possible consequences arising out of any suggestion or action contained in this book to any person reading or following the information in this book.

The authors have sought to trace ownership and, when necessary, obtain permission for quotations included in this book. Occasionally they have been unable to determine or locate the author of a quote. In such instances, if an author of a quotation wishes to contact the authors, he or she should contact them through the publisher.

Book Design by Bonni Leon-Berman

Library of Congress Cataloging in Publication Data
Chodakowski, Ann Fox.
Living on a shoestring / Ann Fox Chodakowski and Susan Fox Wood.
p.   cm.
Includes bibliographical references.
ISBN 0-440-50806-1
1. Finance, Personal.   2. Saving and thrift.   3. Home economics.   I. Wood, Susan Fox.   II. Title.
HG179.C5556   1998
332.024—dc21   97-22818
                                                            CIP

Printed in the United States of America
Published simultaneously in Canada

January 1998

10 9 8 7 6 5 4 3 2 1
BVG

Special thanks go to our Big Sis,
Charlotte Fox Messmer,
for her writing contributions,
and to Nathan W. Vaughn, A.A.S.,
for his illustrations.

To our families, who ate a lot of macaroni and cheese
during the writing of our book . . .

Nathan, our son and artist
Emily, our daughter and diligent worker
Holley, our daughter and little fashion consultant
Alex, husband and financial "bailer-outer!"
Steve, husband and video wiz
Big Sis, Charlotte, for her faith in us!

To our parents, William and (the late) Imogene Fox
for their examples of "living on a shoestring"

Foremost, to God, who gave us strength to carry on
during the tightwad years.
We thank you all . . . and that's the truth.

TO OUR READERS

This book is not for you if you have too much
money in the bank.

You will only find this book *absurd*.

Instead, this book is for the woman who needs all the help
she can get and will go to almost any length to save money
for her family!!!

We dedicate this book to all women who laugh at the "only
$125" outfits on TV shows and to those women who take
pride in looking great for $10 or less.

To our fellow "Tightwad Sisters," we salute you and
hope this book helps you survive life!

—The Tightwad Twins
Cheap and Proud of It!

The Tale of the Tightwad Twins

ONCE UPON A TIME, a set of identical twins was born. They grew up in a loving home with a big sister and brother, a hardworking father, and a mother who raised them "on a shoestring."

Because this family lived on a very tight budget, the twins grew up knowing the value of a dollar. Later in their lives, they had to raise their children alone on a budget. The twins remembered some of their parents' money tips and used them during their hard times. Eventually, they remarried and their husbands encouraged

them to write down some of their "cheap
tricks" and share them with other women.

The twins were not fancy twins. They did
every page of their mail-order manual
themselves, and it was hard! They got on TV
all by themselves and made friends with
Maury, Crook and Chase, and many others.
Women loved their manual of tips and
tightwad jokes and eventually a fancy
publisher named Bantam Doubleday Dell
bought their book!

The twins went on to appear on more
television and radio and to live happily
ever after, knowing in their hearts that
they had done their best and had used their
material blessings well and very wisely.

They also knew that some people would not understand their tightwad ways because some had not been poor enough to realize the value of their book . . . but that was okay.

The twins' mother had died early in their lives. They dedicated their manual to her and to their father. They were the first to give the twins the prescription for being a tightwad and thus the ability to withstand hard times.

. . . And that's the truth.

contents

shoestring living

S Saving Time—Your Most Precious Asset

H Holiday Tips

O Old Rubbish into New Treasures

E Entertaining and Exchanges

S Secondhand Clothes

T Tips for Everyday Living

R Recipes and Food Savers

I Ideas for Children's Rooms

N Nuggets of Wisdom

G Games

YOU KNOW YOU'RE A TIGHTWAD...

...IF YOUR TOUCH-UP PAINT FOR YOUR CAR IS MADE BY REVLON.

Saving Time—Your Most Precious Asset

H
O
E
S
T
R
I
N
G

Nowadays in our world, we are all so busy trying to survive that we often forget about the most important things. Today's woman is often trying to balance a job, a house, children, and the countless errands that come with these responsibilities. The load she carries is for her family, but because the commodity of time is so limited, she doesn't have enough for herself or for just plain being with her family in the personal sense.

Getting organized can save time. Here are few ideas for getting your act together!

one of our secrets is to color-code! Don't laugh! It really works! Matter of fact, our mama use to color-code us. We were identical twins and nobody could tell us apart—that is, except Mama. One time she and Daddy had to go on a trip and Mama left us with Aunt Sarie. Mama had put a blue ribbon on one of us and red one on the other one. Twenty minutes after arriving at Aunt Sarie's that stupid Cousin Con had ripped both the ribbons out of our hair. Aunt Sarie went the whole week without knowing which of us was which. Of course, she told Mama we lost those ribbons the first few minutes we were there! She still doesn't know which one of us put the shaving cream in Cousin Con's Sunday-go-to-meetin' shoes!

If we can't glue it,

Assign **different-colored towel sets** to each member of the family. When you see that towel on the bathroom floor, you'll know who the guilty one is. Knock 50 cents off their allowance, unless it was your husband. If that is the case, you can hide his remote control.

When cleaning up baby, use **ONE COLOR FOR GOO** on the face and **another color for the other end.** It's best not to get the colors mixed up.

Try using dark-colored hand towels for the kiddies to keep stains to a minimum. Another good idea is leaving one near the back door for wiping Spot's feet.

Two different-colored diaper pails placed in the closet for dirty clothes will save time on laundry day. One color for whites, the other for the colored clothes.

Hang each child's clothes on the colored hanger that corresponds to that child. When clothing gets in the wrong closet you can tell at a glance. Saves time looking for lost items.

To divide a closet between two children who share a room, paint one side of the closet one color and the other side another color. You can tell a glance which one of the little darlings left his or her clothes on the closet floor.

Sorting the laundry will go faster if you use *permanent markers* to code each child's clothing. This is a great system if you have two children who wear close to the same size. Put a dot on

we don't do it!

the toe of the socks and a dot on the label of the shirts and another one on the inside waistband of the pants. Be sure to tell the kids their colors.

Next to those hateful little Barbie shoes, most

mothers hate puzzle pieces! When the kiddies get a new puzzle, put a colored dot on the back of each piece. Later, when they have mixed all their puzzles up, you will be able to tell what piece goes to which puzzle. Isn't this a neat idea!

We are big believers in having a big wall calendar. Assign each member of the family a color. At a glance you will be able to spot Bobby's Cub Scout meeting, Mary's ballet lesson, your dental appointment.

TIE THOSE COLORED PENS TO THE WALL. We don't want people using the wrong colored pen because they couldn't find theirs.

In order to seek one's own direction, one must simplify the mechanics of ordinary, everyday life. Plato

If we have to sew it,

If you use a **red pen** each time you record checks that are **tax-related,** at the end of the year when you file your tax return, they will be easy to spot.

Get yourself some colored **FILE FOLDERS.** Use a red one for bills to pay, a green one for medical, insurance, etc., forms, and a yellow one for paid bill receipts.

Give each family member a color and file folder, which you can use to file medical records and school information.

When organizing *grocery coupons,* use colored envelopes for each category. Green for soaps and cleaning supplies, blue for bread and cereals, and red for canned goods.

Don't forget to make a color-key card and post it near your wall calendar so each member of the family knows how your system works.

before you and your family can be more productive at keeping the house in order, you need to first start with a "**house clearing**." Get rid of the clutter and dirt and your future housework will take less time. Here's how!

TAKE A WALK THROUGH THE HOUSE.
Figure out what jobs you want to tackle and what equipment you need to do that job.

we'd rather throw it!

If it is a real time-consuming task like cleaning the carpet, get that over with first.

Once you decide what needs to be done in each room, get your cleaning supplies together. Put them in a bucket and carry them room to room.

Don't overwhelm yourself, it will only lead to frustration. Begin each room with an easy job so that you can see the results instantly. Declutter the top shelf in the closet. Now, that wasn't so bad, and because that one shelf is clean and in order it will spur you on toward your goal.

Some people don't have clutter or dirt in their house. We decided to dislike them, mainly because we have clutter and dirt in our houses. Of course, if our husbands lived in the barn most of the time, our houses might look a little different.

Get your clean-up-the-house clothes on. No sense in being miserable while you're doing this task.

The old adage "Do what you are doing" is a good motto to go by. Don't be distracted by nonemergencies. Turn the TV off! If you have to have some sort of sound, turn on the radio to "easy listening" or rock 'n' roll. You can either *jitterbug or waltz your way through your work.* And if people stop in, tell them the kitchen floor is wet, which will protect your food supply, and hand them a pair of rubber gloves and cleaning rag. They'll be gone in about 5 minutes. No, 3 minutes.

Writing down what you buy

Toss, recycle, or give away as much clutter as possible. If you're not using it or enjoying it, why are you letting it live rent-free in your house?

Hard by the yard, cinch by the inch!   *Us*

Arrange things according to how frequently they are used. You can put the Christmas decorations on the back shelf. Take the time now to label your containers. If you do it right now, it will save you time in the future.

We would suggest you get the **worst rooms first.** In most homes, these are the bathrooms and kitchen. Work around the room instead of crisscrossing: saves steps and lugging cleaning supplies back and forth. Besides, you can look over your shoulder at the clean part and **SMILE.**

If you really don't know where to begin in one of these "worst" rooms, here are some steps that might help. Let's take the kitchen.

Remove the curtains and launder them.

Look at space on your *countertops*; reserve that space for items used on a daily basis.

will shock you to the sky!

Remove from cabinets the small appliances and dishes that you never use. Include them in your next **GARAGE SALE.**

Clean out the pantry, put together duplicate packages, label containers. The last time we cleaned out our pantry, we found three boxes of spaghetti! Guess what we had for dinner.

Spray the oven with oven cleaner. While it's doing

its thing, get the ammonia out and clean the range hood.

Clean the inside of your refrigerator with baking soda and warm water. Clean the outside of the refrigerator with glass cleaner. That will leave a nice shine on it.

Remember the oven? Go back to it and finish the cleaning.

If you have a microwave oven, clean it with the same baking soda and warm water you used on the refrigerator.

Wash and wipe down the cabinet doors and woodwork. Give the **TRASH CAN** a good disinfecting.

And last, scrub and wax the floor.

Now, you may crump in the corner and, with a smile on your face, admire your clean kitchen. You may dismember any child or husband that dares to make a mess in that room!

Beware of small expenses;

She watches carefully all that goes on throughout her household, and is never lazy.
Proverbs 31:27

to control "mealtime madness"—

For us cooking is the easy part, it's the menu planning, the grocery shopping, the putting away, and the cleanup that are the chores. The secret? Get organized!

Keep on index cards ten of your can't-miss dinners.
Include the whole menu: salad, side dishes, beverage, and dessert. On the back of the card list the grocery items it takes to prepare that dinner. Take the card with you when you do your grocery shopping. Better yet, tell hubby it is time to get up from his blue recliner and to put the remote control down and go grocery shopping!

When you make meatloaf, soups, macaroni and cheese, stews and casseroles, **MAKE DOUBLE OR TRIPLE BATCHES.** Put them in containers that can go from the freezer to the microwave or oven.

a small leak can sink a big ship!

If possible, precook meals or parts of meals on the weekend. Make your sauces, if pasta is on the menu for the week, peel and chop veggies, etc. Big Sis stews a whole chicken, picks it off the bones and freezes it in individual freezer bags. She uses the chicken for casseroles or soups and even tosses it with pasta and a sauce. Look for some of her mouthwatering dishes in the recipe section.

The sooner you get going, the farther ahead you get! Us

Sometimes we all get so tired, we can't even take something out of the freezer. For those times, spend the little extra money and *order takeout.* Chinese goes a long way. Rice is nice! Order a pizza and toss a salad while you're waiting for the delivery. Stop by the deli on the way home from work and get one of those rotisserie chickens; when you get home, brush it with some honey mustard, pop it in the broiler for a few minutes. Steam some chopped-up veggies to go with it. They are already chopped and in the freezer aren't they?

for all **working moms,** get your morning act together the night before.

Decide what you are to wear and lay it out. Dress, shoes, stockings, underwear. The whole ball of wax!

Every little bit helps;

Pack your purse or briefcase, and are the car keys on the special lit-tle hook by the door? Find them now! Has the car got gas in it? Why didn't you stop today before you came home from work?

Lay the kiddies' clothes out. Make sure the kids have their homework done and that it's with their coat or jacket by the front door. Do they need money for lunch or whatever? Put it with the jacket and homework. Now!

Set the table for breakfast. Put the cereal in the bowls, cover them with a saucer or a piece of plastic wrap, pour the juice in the glasses, put them in the refrigerator. Is the kitchen timer out and on the table? When you set it the next morning and it goes off, the kids know it's time to get dressed!

If your children take their lunch to school, **PACK** it the **night before** and put it in the refrigerator! Take it out of the refrigerator when you get the children's breakfast juice. Put the lunch with the jacket, homework, and money by the front door.

And remember–

The only thing improved by anger is the arch on a cat's back!　*Us*

a mansion is built one brick at a time.

Always have a backup plan for a late baby-sitter or a sick school-age child. ALWAYS!

And remember–

> *A hundred years from now*
> *. . .it will not matter what my bank account was,*
> *the sort of house I lived in, or the kind of car*
> *I drove—*
> *. . .but the world may be different because I was*
> *important in the*
> *life of a child.*
>
> *Unknown*

Apple-type storage boxes are great to use in bedrooms and closets and look **rustic and cute** for other things in other areas of your house.

The space going from the bottom of your kitchen cabinets down to the top of your counter can be used as storage. **YOU CAN USE WOODEN CRATES,** like the ones supermarkets get their veggies in, or plastic ones, which are super cheap and come in all different colors. Stack dishes in them, or small appliances.

Clean out that closet you have been avoiding and turn it into a "me" space. A quiet study area with a table top and shelves. One easy-to-install desk can be made from a slab of wood or laminate-covered wood supported by cleats or brackets nailed to the wall. If you want to get fancy, install mirrors on the back wall and use glass shelves to complement. Add a lamp, a cupful of

If we can't do it fast,

pencils, and a pad of paper, and write the Great American Novel, or write in a journal, or clip coupons and recipes, it doesn't matter; the point is, **IT'S YOUR SPACE.**

Set up a *coupon file* that can be carried with you in your car or in your purse always. This will hold *all* of your coupons. Fill your organizer with every available coupon you can get your hands on. Newspapers and magazines are the most accessible. Most grocery stores have coupon bins for customers to help themselves.

Set up a file in a drawer or a box in your house with sections divided into groups such as **cleaners, paper products, beverages, meats, dog food, medicines, personal hygiene, dressings and sauces, miscellaneous (batteries, etc.), vegetables/side dishes, condiments,** etc. This will be your rebate file and also the file you will hold for your cash register receipts and UPC labels that you will cut off purchases. Put your UPC labels in an envelope and write on the outside of the envelope what the product was and the size. Keep your receipt with the UPC symbols if your cash register receipt is not the kind that itemizes.

Save empty egg cartons for your *Christmas ornaments.* They store nicely and are protected and organized. The top may not close completely, but a rubber band over it will still protect and secure the larger ornaments.

Shoe box lids make spool thread organizers. Lay them on their sides to see their colors and place in a drawer or on a shelf. They will not roll around so much.

then we won't last!

Use the inexpensive **plastic pencil boxes** for storage in the car or the house. Great for cassette tapes. Some boxes can hold CDs.

Egg cartons organize buttons, earrings, etc. Paint if you desire.

Always keep a closet with boxes labeled "share," "sell," or "store."

Used silverware trays are great for organizing anything.

Pick up **USED MUFFIN TINS** for storing nails, buttons, sewing, paper clips, etc. These can also be painted.

To make containers for small, loose items such as jewelry, cover a *tennis ball can* or a potato chip can with contact paper, leftover wallpaper, or wrapping paper.

S O E S T R I N G

Holiday Tips

YOU KNOW YOU'RE A TIGHTWAD...

...IF WAL-MART SENDS YOU A CHRISTMAS CARD!

Christmas

'Twas the night before Christmas, when all through the house

Not a creature was stirring—not even a mouse;

The stockings were hung by the chimney with care,

In hopes that St. Nicholas soon would be there.

Clement Clarke Moore

every year when we see the giant balloons rise above the televised Thanksgiving Day parade, our hearts skip a beat at the realization that we are once again about to be plunged into our annual holiday *hysteria.* We had promised ourselves, as we do every year, that by July we would have all the presents made or bought and wrapped! Only in our dreams . . .

Somehow we have the misbegotten notion that if just one of our Christmas traditions is let go, the whole family will be struck by lightning and it will definitely be our fault. Traditions are sacred: the Christmas cards, the visit to Santa, decorating the tree, making the cookies, the Christmas Eve church service, presents for everyone in the entire state, stockings hung by the chimney with care . . .

As our family grew, we finally had to take ourselves in hand and admit that we couldn't do everything. We told our children and husbands that the "S" on our sweatshirt did not stand for Supermom,

Slave, Stupid, or Simple, but for "Serene." Of course, they really believed this! Here are a few of our "Serene" tips to help you, we hope, cope with this busy season.

Aunt Sarie starts baking Christmas cookies around Halloween; by Christmas every surface in her kitchen is covered with mounds of cookies in a kaleidoscope of shapes and colors. Groan! Limit yourself to two kinds of cookies and make triple batches of each, or have a cookie exchange in your neighborhood or office or church. An exchange works like this: Everyone brings 6 dozen cookies, plus one cookie for everybody on the guest list to taste. When you leave, depending on the number of people invited, you leave with dozens of cookies. Tell Aunt Sarie that you baked them all and watch her turn green. P.S. Have all the guests at the cookie exchange bring a copy of their recipes with them!

What are you going to do with all of those cookies? First, save some for the family to eat. The rest are gifts: teachers, Sunday school teachers, those special neighbors, co-workers, your boss, your minister, your friends, etc.

Containers for those gifts of cookies: Christmas trays or tins from the $ store or thrift store, Mason jars, and pretty little baskets. Line the container with a Christmas napkin or use a piece of red-and-white or green-and-white-checked fabric cut with pinking shears. Put the cookies in, trim with a bright Christmas ribbon, pine cones, candy sticks, Christmas tree ornaments, or whatever else strikes your fancy. Now that wasn't too bad, was it?

Christmas is that refreshing day when the kids get up early without turning on the TV.

Finding time to get the Christmas cards ready is often the last straw. Some of our friends have sensibly done away with this custom. Here's what you can do: Forget about it or have the children make them. To us, there is nothing more precious than receiving a **Christmas card made out of green or red construction paper** and decorated with a stick reindeer or a cottonball Santa Claus.

We all have far-flung friends or relatives who should be sent lengthy personal letters. Write them **after Christmas when your sanity has returned.** Just get it done before Valentine's Day!

To make inexpensive cards, get some blank note cards and some self-sticking red and green coding dots. Form a wreath or swag with the dots. Write a verse and sign your name in gold pen!

the kiddies are out of school for the holidays, they are bored, they are asking every five minutes, **"How much longer?"** You are patient and loving with them and you have started to grind your

generates an income of its own.

teeth in your sleep. Have courage, we have been there! Here are a few ideas for keeping your children busy while you are busy, and maybe we can save on future dental bills for you.

Cover the kitchen table with plastic—a garbage bag split open will do the trick—tape the plastic with masking tape around the edges so that the plastic will not scoot. For each child fix a small basket, coffee can, or plastic container. Fill each container with a pair of round-nose scissors, a pencil, some colored markers or crayons, school glue, bits and pieces of ribbon, twine, yarn, rickrack, lace, big buttons, and anything else you can think of. Give each child a couple sheets of construction paper and some plain white paper. **Decorate the tree with their creations!**

For snowflakes, draw around a plate or saucer on plain white paper. Cut out the circle and fold it in half. Fold the half into thirds. Make the creases sharp along the folds. Draw a pretty design on the folded paper and then carefully cut out the design. Now, cut some circles and triangles along the two straight edges. Cut big ones and small ones. The more cuts you make, the lacier your snowflake will be. Open the snowflake very carefully or it will tear. Poke a hole at the top of the snowflake and put a ribbon or piece of twine through it for a hanger.

FROM A CARDBOARD EGG CARTON, cut out one of the cups that hold the eggs. You can leave the edge straight or cut a pretty scallop around the top of the cup. Poke a small hole on either side of the cup and thread a piece of ribbon or yarn

It's not how much you make,

through the holes for the handle. Be sure and tie a knot in the end of your ribbon or yarn on the inside of the cup so that it will not pull through the holes. On a sheet of paper, trace around a cup or glass to make a circle. With a crayon or marker, draw a thick scalloped edge around the circle—don't forget to draw your scalloped edge on the other side of the paper too! Cut the scalloped circle out and put a dab of glue in the bottom of your egg cup. Press the circle inside the cup. Hold it in place until the glue is dry. Usually, one chorus of "Jingle Bells" will be enough time for the glue to dry. Fill your little basket with jelly beans or Christmas candy and hang it on the tree or give it to a special friend.

No day is complete until you've heard the laughter of a child.

For this tree decoration you will need a bag of **bite-size pretzel twists.** On wax paper lay six of the little pretzels in a circle. Glue the pretzels together where they touch. When the glue is dry, make another circle of pretzels right on top of your first circle! When the glue is dry, this one usually takes one verse of "Here Comes Santa Claus," add a red or green loop for hanging on the tree. Remember not to eat the pretzels once they have glue on them or you'll get a tummy ache or, worse, you'll never be able to eat again because your teeth will be glued shut!

Here's a real cutie and lots of fun to make. Again, we are going to use pretzels, but the stick kind. *Little log cabins!* Save from school several of those little milk cartons. Wash the carton and glue the opening together. Cut the pretzels—these are the logs—to fit all sides of the milk carton. Cover the carton with ready-made frosting and press the "little logs" onto the frosting. For the roof shingles use some frosted bite-size shredded wheat cereal. Use the frosted, it looks like snow! *Make a little village* of your tiny cabins.

From last year's Christmas cards cut out designs, glue them to circles or stars cut from red or green construction paper. Poke a hole at the top to thread a piece of ribbon or yarn through, knot the ribbon, and hang on the tree.

We've saved the best for last. Mix 1 cup flour, $^1/_4$ cup salt and $^1/_3$ cup water in a bowl. Stir until it is well mixed, press the clay between your fingers to get out any lumps. If the clay feels dry or crumbly, add a few drops of water. If it feels too mushy, add a bit of flour. Store the "Goofy Dough" in a plastic bag in the refrigerator, but let it warm to room temperature when you are ready to use it. Let's use it! Roll out the dough on wax paper and use Christmas cookie cutters to make the shapes you want. While the ornaments are still soft, press a paper clip into the top of each. Make sure the top of the clip sticks out over the top of the figure. This will be for your hanger. Let the little figures dry for 2 to 3 days. Be patient! Color them with acrylic paint (that's water-base, Mom). When figures are dry, brush them with a coat of clear nail polish. String colored yarn through the paper-clip loops, and hang the ornaments from the Christmas tree.

If we can't glue it,

Don't forget some of the **simplest things** that you might have around the house often **make the best tree decorations.** String popcorn, spools of thread, beads from broken necklaces....Make garlands of macaroni, painted with old nail polish; dust with glitter....Glue strips of bright paper in interlocking circles to form a chain.

here are a few tightwad tips for decorating the outside of your home. Does it ever end? We still have to do the inside!

To welcome the holidays, light your walkway or driveway with **glowing homemade luminaries.** Use medium-size brown paper bags. Roll the top of the bag down to form a cuff or two; this helps the bag to stand up. Draw a simple design such as a Christmas tree or star on the bags. Punch holes along the lines with a paper-hole punch. Fill the bags with about 2 inches of sand and center a small votive candle in the bottom. When lit, the flickering candlelight shines through your cutout design. P.S. Don't worry about the bag catching fire; the candle burns down to the sand and the flame dies.

Wrap a bunch of boxes with Christmas paper and arrange them in a larger box, covered with red paper, and place on a child's sled, fill in the spaces around the packages with fresh evergreen—which was free because you found it in the woods. Now you have a sleigh that looks like it came out of another time. Well, sort of...You'll like it!

we don't do it!

Cover the mailbox with designs you've cut in self-stick colored plastic, just be sure the box still opens, or the postman will be very upset. (We sure don't want that since the postman is Cousin Con! And…don't forget who his mother is!)

Poke a hole at the top of holiday cookies before you bake and decorate them, then hang them from a ribbon in a window (indoors, facing out).

Buy plastic foam canes, or cut them from foam sheets. Stripe with red and white outdoor ribbon wound around them at an angle. Hang them from the trees.

Go back into the woods and get some more *evergreen stuff* and make garlands to go around your windows; add strings of outdoor lights to the garlands.

Spray-paint some wooden birdhouses red and others gold to hang from trees, or line them up along an outside windowsill. Add some holly sprigs or evergreen sprays between the houses.

Hang "tin" ornaments (cut from foil pie plates) instead of lights on a bush near the house.

Tie outdoor lights to trees and posts with **old nylon stockings.**

Decorate outside doors with Christmas trees cut from white plastic foamboard. Attach the trees with double-sided tape, then pin on bright ornaments and garlands of beads.

If we have to sew it,

Never mistake knowledge for wisdom. One helps you make a living; the other helps you make a life.   Sandra Carey

inside the house . . .

If you are a naturalist, like Big Sis, you can create some great decorations that are simple, and best of all most of the materials are *free!* Nature provides an abundance of choices. For fresh foliage you cannot beat holly branches with bright red berries, magnolia branches, pine, spruce, and other types of evergreen. If your taste leans toward country or traditional, fill crocks, vases, or pitchers with water and boughs and place them around the house. Here are a few ideas.

For your kitchen table or dining area an old pitcher or coffeepot filled with holly branches with a red ribbon tied on its handle all sitting atop an old quilt or quilt remnant is a setting right out of *Country Home.* If you don't have an old quilt or remnant, use a square or rectangle of red-and-white-checked fabric; cut the edges of the fabric with pinking shears.

To have a *nature Christmas tree,* hang apples, pears, and pine cones from its branches. Use ribbon or jute twine for the hangers. Place bird nests filled with moss and acorns among the tree branches. Use dried flowers, such as Queen Anne's lace, to add another dimension to your nature tree. Usually dried flowers and grasses do not need a hanger, they will cling naturally to the branches of the tree. For **a top ornament,** cut a star out of a brown paper sack and glue it to cardboard so it will stand up, or cut your star out of a tin pie pan or put a fake cardinal bird at the top. Look at the $ store for other natural looking birds and animals.

Poke oranges with a meat fork, put whole cloves in the holes. Fill a bowl or crock with the clove studded fruit and smell that wonderful scent of cloves and oranges all the holiday season.

Poor is the man who cannot enjoy the simple things of life.

if you like to decorate with a little more sparkle than the "natural" look, then stay tuned. This section is for you.

Again, gather all that free stuff from nature, but this time we are going to gild the lily.

Beware of small expenses;

Spray-paint your pine cones gold, silver, or white. While they are still wet, sprinkle with gold or silver glitter. When they have dried, hang them on the tree with a gold, silver, red, or green narrow ribbon.

After you pick Queen Anne's lace, spray it, back and front, with white spray paint and sprinkle silver glitter on while they are wet. Place the stems through cardboard to dry. On the tree they will look *like sparkling snowflakes!*

Spray-paint silver or gold the most **tacky fake fruit** you can find. Look at thrift stores for the absolute cheapest price. You don't care what it looks like since you are going to **paint it!** Put your "new" fruit into a glass bowl, a basket you've sprayed white or gold, or use a pretty china bowl. Set it on a mirror in the middle of your table and place a ring of candles around it. This is a real sparkler with the lights turned down low.

Some people treat the world as though they have a spare in the trunk.

Us

For a great wreath over a door or on a wall or over the fireplace, use a **Styrofoam wreath,** attach fresh cranberries to the foam wreath with toothpicks, add a bright gold or green bow; for a very special effect spray a little fake snow here and there on the cranber-

a small leak can sink a big ship!

ries. When Christmas is over, save your bow until next year, and hang the cranberry wreath on a tree outside for the birds. They will love it!

LET'S DO THE TREE ALL IN WHITE. Use the dried flowers that we painted white, add painted white pine cones, holly and berries, apples, pears, and nuts. Add white doves all over the tree; these are super cheap at the $ store and even cheaper if you bought them after Christmas last year! For the top ornament use a single white dove or a wide white velvet ribbon with its streamers left long so they flow down the tree, or a star of gold or silver embellished with glitter or fake shiny beads.

So you don't want white. Paint all the props we've been telling you about a shade of soft mauve or pale pink. Martha Stewart did hers **in pale greens.** We saw that on TV.

In our next life we are going to be Martha Stewart. Well, maybe a hillbilly version! At least a Tightwad version. Oh, who cares!

Make tiny bells from **empty restaurant cream containers—** tie red ribbons through the hole and hang on door. Roll in glue and glitter for a brighter look.

Spray-paint **old artificial fruit or flowers** with gold for Christmas or for a classy touch.

Fill a silver or crystal clear bowl with Christmas balls and mingle with strings of small white lights for a centerpiece.

Every little bit helps;

You can buy rough-texture angels, Nativity scenes, or other figures at $ stores and spray-paint them gold or white for an **expensive-looking decoration.**

Make your own decorative Christmas tree cake.
For a square cake, cut it in half, making two triangles and add M & M's for ornaments. For a rectangle cake, cut away pieces making a tall Christmas tree. Add candy "ornaments" and raisins or chocolate chips for the "trunk."

Halloween

Once upon a midnight dreary, while I pondered, weak and weary,
Over many a quaint and curious volume of forgotten lore—
While I nodded, nearly napping, suddenly there came a tapping,
As of some one gently rapping, rapping at my chamber door.
"'Tis some visitor," I muttered, "tapping at my chamber door—
Only this and nothing more."

Edgar Allan Poe

boo! Here are some monstrous ideas for Halloween!

Instead of cutting the top off when you **carve your pumpkin, cut the bottom off.** No more reaching inside burning your hand while lighting the pumpkin. Just light the candle and put the pumpkin over it!

a mansion is built one brick at a time.

Here's an easier way to carve a jack-o-lantern. Find a pattern of what you want to carve. Children's books and coloring books are a great source for this. Lay the pattern on the pumpkin, poke a series of holes, use a nail, along the pattern lines. When you remove the pattern, just connect the dots and carve away!

To remove the pulp and seeds from the pumpkin. Use an ice-cream scoop; the handle is shorter and the bowl of the scoop is deeper than that of a big cooking spoon.

Remember how to roast the seeds? Spread them on a cookie sheet and spray with nonstick cooking spray. Bake at 350 degrees until they are light brown, sprinkle with salt, and then stuff yourself.

Instead of a candle inside of your pumpkin, **use a flashlight** in the bottom of the jack-o-lantern or line the bottom of the pumpkin with aluminum foil and put a string of tiny exterior Christmas tree lights inside, poke a hole out the back of the pumpkin for the cord.

Here's a **SCARY HALLOWEEN PUNCH.** The kids love this! Fill a disposable plastic glove, not the kind with powder inside, with water or ginger ale; tie the top of the water-filled glove closed, and freeze. When you are ready for your "hand," dip the frozen glove in warm water for just a minute and peel off the glove. Now, for the black punch for the hand to float in: one package each of unsweetened grape and orange Kool-Aid, 2 cups of sugar, and 3 quarts of cold water; then add 1 chilled bottle of ginger ale just before serving.

If we can't do it fast,

To make Halloween dinner really special, **serve a stew in a hollowed-out pumpkin!** Cut a large slice off the top, remove all the slimy stuff and seeds, rinse out, and sprinkle with salt and pepper. Put the pumpkin on foil with the top you cut off beside it, and bake at 350 degrees until it is fork tender but not soft: about 45 minutes. Put your heated stew inside and put the top on. By now the kids are jumping up and down and squealing.

Make a centerpiece for your Halloween table by hollowing out a pumpkin and filling it with *flowers, real or fake.*

For dessert serve ice cream or orange sherbet in scooped-out oranges. Draw a funny or scary face on them with a felt marker.

Use one-gallon ice-cream containers that come with handles for a trick-or-treat bucket.

Here's a goody our kids loved! Take a clear plastic glove and put a piece of corn candy in the bottom of each finger (these look like fingernails), then fill the fingers and the glove with popcorn! Tie the top of the glove with a ribbon, and for an extra touch, put one of those fake black plastic spider rings on the ring finger. A package of those silly rings cost about 50 cents at the $ store.

let's get on our costumes!

Use a green plastic garbage bag, belted in the middle, for a **Robin Hood** costume. Add tights and V-shaped hat out of a brown paper sack.

then we won't last!

Use an orange plastic leaf bag, cut a hole for each of the child's legs at the bottom of the bag. Once it is on, stuff with crumpled newspapers. You can either cut armholes and gather and tie the bag around your child's neck or belt the top under his arms. With black tights and an orange beanie on the head, you have the **"BIG" PUMP-KIN!**

One year one of ours went as Robin Hood, and Cousin Con went along dressed as a tree. He wore long underwear and stapled leaves all over his long johns and had some kind of branch with leaves on his head. Said he was Robin's Sherwood Forest! We hate to admit it, but that was a good idea and a sight to behold! We wonder if Aunt Sarie saw him before he left. We think not. She wouldn't think it "appropriate" for a postman to wear such a getup!

For a last-minute costume for a little girl, use a green T-shirt and tights and necklace of paper petals, using either crepe paper or construction paper. She becomes a flower! Add a little hat for her head as the center of the flower.

For an **instant rabbit** costume, use a hooded sweat shirt, attach construction paper ears, glue cottonballs around the face on the hood, and make a great big pom-pom ball and pin at the seat of the pants in the rear; paint whiskers and pink nose on the face.

For an **instant gypsy** you need a vest, a white blouse, a bright-colored long skirt, and plenty of gaudy costume jewelry. Add a scarf tied to one side of the head, and a big hoop earring on one ear. For a tambourine, take two paper plates, facing each other, fill with dried beans or gravel for the rattle, staple edges of plates together, tie a few long ribbons to the plate and let them hang down. All of the clothing can be found at a thrift store cheapo.

To make a **robot,** cover two cardboard rectangles, as tall as your child from shoulder to shin, with tinfoil. Staple wide ribbon or welting to the top corners of the front cardboard, drape ribbon or welting over the shoulders to the back cardboard, and staple. You might want to staple another tie on the cardboard under the arms to keep it from flopping. Make a helmet out of tinfoil.

For a quick butterfly costume, use a floral or colored pillowcase. Cut holes for head and arms and use foamboard or cardboard for butterfly wings. Paint the wings; when they're dry attach the wings to the pillowcase with wide ribbon and fabric tape. Use pipe cleaners glued to a headband for antennae.

A round cake with orange frosting makes a great **Halloween pumpkin cake.** Decorate with candy or raisins or chocolate chips.

There has not been a single day since the world began when the sun was not shining. The trouble has been with our vision.

Unknown

generates an income of its own.

To decorate tables for the holidays use this simple and cheap trick. Sprinkle candy corn for Halloween or fall, Christmas candy during the holidays, flower petals during spring, and so forth.

Easter

here's how to make an Easter basket with real grass.

Line a pretty basket with aluminum foil or plastic wrap, add a couple of quarts of a sterile medium—perlite or vermiculite, which can be bought at any store ending in "mart"—and a handful of "wheat seeds," which can be bought real cheap at a seed store or nursery. You don't have to plant the seeds, just scatter them on top of the medium—let's right now call "medium" *dirt*—and water the basket until water comes almost to the top of the dirt. Drape a layer of plastic loosely over the basket to keep the seeds moist while they sprout. Wheat seeds grow really fast; usually within a day or two they have sprouted, and soon after green leaves will appear and then it will grow at a rate of more than an inch a day! Remove the plastic and place basket in a sunny window.

You won't have to water the grass again. It takes about a week to grow lush 6- to 8-inch-tall grass. So-o-o, if you plant the seed a week before Easter, you should have a basketful of grass by Easter Sunday.

It's not how much you make,

Put your usual items in the basket: eggs, candy and bunnies or chicks, depending on the child. If he's like Cousin Con, you might want to keep it for yourself and use it for the table centerpiece on Easter Sunday.

If you are a doodler, always scribbling on notepads and scraps of paper, then you've definitely got to get a life! And while you are at it **DO SOME DOODLES ON EASTER EGGS.** Boil the eggs first, then draw rows of playful, childlike flowers or dots or bows or teeny bunnies with multicolored felt-tip markers. The result is pretty eggs without all that messy dye. Which is definitely a mother's nightmare unless you let the kids do their dye job in Uncle Ed's barn. He won't mind, but he's not exactly in love with the idea.

To make a cute "egg tree" tramp back out to the woods again and this time find an interestingly shaped twig, one with several little branches springing from a straight center trunk. Spray-paint it white, pale pink, or pale yellow. Fill a flowerpot, a clean clay or a pretty plastic one, with Stryofoam. Stand the painted "tree" in the pot. Attach little tiny plastic eggs with ribbon and hang them from the branches of the tree. Add moss to the top of the pot to cover the foam. Use dried Spanish moss, though we like to use the real thing. You know, that green velvety stuff that grows everywhere you don't want it to.

The children will love making these Easter Egg Pigs. You will need 1 hard-boiled egg for each pig and 5 small gumdrops for each pig. (Be sure to use fresh gumdrops. Stale ones won't stick properly.) Cut a thin slice from the flat end of each gumdrop. Save the cut-off bits. Press 4 gumdrops in place to form the pig's legs. Cut the fifth gum-

it's how much you keep!

drop in half lengthwise and use the gumdrop halves for the pig's ears. Cut eyes, nose, and tail from the saved bits of gumdrop. Press in place. You can draw a smile on your pig's face with a felt-tipped marker.

I remember one time when Cousin Con was a little boy, he put freckles on his pig. Aunt Sarie thought that was really a very creative idea. If anybody else had put freckles on their pig, Aunt Sarie would want to know, "What are those funny-looking dots?" Then she'd go tell your mother that **therapy** should definitely be a consideration.

Here are some things you can use besides baskets for your children's Easter goodies.

A child's sandpail: fill the scoop of the little plastic shovel that usually comes with the pail with jelly beans, held in place with a piece of plastic wrap.

Small plastic paint buckets come in great Easter colors: aqua, hot pink, yellow, and even orange and purple. Fill with paper grass and tie a big bow on the handle. These buckets sell for less than a dollar!

Use an old straw hat. Turn it upside down, fill with fake grass, and staple a ribbon-covered cardboard handle to the sides of the hat. Make a nosegay of fake posies and attach to the handle to hide your staples.

If we have to sew it,

While traveling along the road of life, enjoy the going and stop thinking so fiercely about getting there.

us

Valentine's Day

valentine's day wouldn't be Valentine's Day without lots and lots of hearts. Here's how to make them in all shapes and sizes.

Cut a square from a piece of construction paper or wrapping paper. Fold the paper square in half. Draw half a heart on it and cut it out. Of course, when you open the paper you will have a perfect heart! You can make your hearts skinny or fat; teeny hearts or giant ones; the edges can be smooth or curly. Paste a little pink heart on a big purple one; a whole lot of little red ones on a big pink one. Let your imagination soar. This can be a great time spent with the children; fix a special snack while you are working and, most of all, listen to those little voices while they totally destroy a whole pack of construction paper.

we'd rather throw it!

To make a **stained-glass heart,** cut another heart out of the middle of a big heart, leave a frame or border of about $^3/_4$ inch and tape different-colored cellophane to the back of the paper heart. Remember, blue cellophane over yellow will give you green, red over yellow will give you orange, and red over blue will give you purple. If you brush a little glue over the cellophane, it will look more like glass. Don't forget your glue goes on white but will dry clear. Now poke a tiny hole at the "V" of your stained-glass heart, thread a string through the hole, and hang the heart up in a window. Wait until you see the sun shine through all those colors!

Cut a potato in half, draw a pattern on the cut surface of each half: a heart, arrow, or flower. With a knife cut away any potato that is not part of the pattern. Cover the raised part, which is your pattern, with a light coat of poster paint. Lightly press your potato onto paper. Use the paper to wrap a gift or to make a card. Let the paint dry and print over it with another color. *Experiment!*

The best and most beautiful things in the world cannot be seen or even touched. They must be felt with the heart.
Helen Keller

Just because you're a tightwad doesn't mean you were born without any taste or imagination. Even **Scarlett O'Hara** made herself a dress out of a curtain!

Thanksgiving

turkey time!

Thanksgiving! For your table on this special day again look to nature for the best decorations and they are *free*. Gather colorful autumn leaves, sprays of evergreen, and pine cones. Using a tray, lay evergreen on first to cover the tray, then arrange small pumpkins, yellow squash, gourds, and apples of red and green, tuck in a pine cone here and there and leaves of all colors, add a few candles, and you've got it!

For napkin rings, wind honeysuckle vine around a glass, tuck the ends in and slip it off the glass. Thread your napkin through the little wreath. Perfect to go with your nature's centerpiece.

If you like a dressier look, spray ears of dried corn, gourds, pine cones, and, yes, even a pumpkin, *gold!* Spray fake apples gold and make a hole in the center of them and use them as candleholders. If they are wobbly, weight them with rocks. Weave a gold ribbon around and in between the candles and your arrangement; leave the tails long so they will spread down the table. For napkin rings, use large gold curtain rings or tie a strip of gold ribbon around the napkin.

will shock you to the sky!

Don't forget to look in the recipe section for some of our favorite economical dishes for Thanksgiving!

Gifts and Giftwraps for All Occasions

here are a few ideas for tightwad gifts.

At the $ store buy a set of baskets, one smaller than the other so that they fit inside each other, fill each basket with a colorful array of hair fixin's: ribbons, ponytail holders, and fancy barrettes—a super gift for a teenage girl.

A winning combination for the *sports buff:* sun visor, sports socks, goggles, baby powder, and a big box of bandages. Adjust the items to the person's particular sport.

Here's a great gift for the serious driver—a car **emergency kit.** Put jumper cables, flares, fix-a-flat stuff, and a flashlight with batteries in a box with a lid that can be stowed in the trunk.

For someone that rides the bus, train, or subway to work, a tote bag with a folding umbrella, a magazine or book, and a little munchie makes a thoughtful gift.

Beware of small expenses;

A picnic basket filled with a checked tablecloth, white napkins, candles and their holders, and a bottle of wine with two wineglasses makes a neat gift for the *romantic couple* on your list. I wonder, can we go on the picnic with them?

THIS IS A REAL CHEAP-AND-EASY ONE.

For the green thumb on your list, put seed packets and a gardening trowel inside a pair of gardening gloves. Tie a big red bow around it and bingo! Another one out of the way!

> The private and personal blessings we enjoy, the blessings of immunity, safeguard, liberty and integrity, deserve the thanksgiving of a whole life.
> *Jeremy Taylor*

Team a bright salad bowl (remember the $ store) with a bottle of olive oil and a bottle of wine vinegar, and you've got a gift to make any **salad lover** happy.

more eleventh-hour gifts.

Travel kit: cosmetics bag with plastic bottles, toothbrush holder, soap, toothpaste, towelettes.

a small leak can sink a big ship!

Writing combo: letter holder, pens, pretty notepaper—plus stamps!

Fix-it: home-repair book (look for this at thrift stores), nails, screws, simple tools, all in a bright plastic pail.

Eat-at-your-desk: mug, tea and coffee bags, can opener, salt and pepper, napkins, and a small thermos.

Dieter's delight: small food-scale, diet recipes and hints, a calorie/fat counter booklet—and throw in some low-cal snacks. Put in a nice basket and tie a bright bow on the handle.

When a friend compliments you on a recipe, you can turn it into a special gift by giving one or more of the ingredients along with a copy of the recipe: spices for a dip, the wine for beef Burgundy, or a special rice for a favorite casserole.

For that *new in-law* in the family, fill an address book with addresses and phone numbers of family and friends; add a special section for birthdays and anniversaries.

By the time you learn all the lessons of life, you're too weak to walk to the head of the class.

Every little bit helps;

The kids will love this one. Roll up a dollar bill and poke it into a balloon. Mail it in a card with instructions to blow up the balloon and then pop it!

When your children receive a gift, take a picture of them playing with it or wearing it and send it as a thank-you note. Even if it is that dumb sweater that Aunt Sarie sent your son. **PINK!** Tell your son if he will stand still for the picture, you will shrink that sweater in the wash; and tell Aunt Sarie that he is growing by leaps and bounds and it just breaks your heart that he can't wear that pretty pink sweater anymore. Your tongue just fell out for fibbin'!

here are a few ideas that will make gift wrapping a little easier.

Simplify the storing of wrapping paper by placing it in a tall wastebasket. With Velcro, attach a bag to the side of the wastebasket for scissors, tape, pen, and labels.

Save wrapping paper after gifts have been opened. Wrinkled paper can be perked up by lightly spraying the wrong side with spray starch and pressing with a warm iron.

Run wrinkled ribbon through a hot curling iron. We love this one!

To make your own ribbon, cut almost any type of fabric into the width and length you need. Press the strips between sheets of wax paper with a hot iron. The wax keeps the strips from unravel-

a mansion is built one brick at a time.

ing and provides enough stiffness for the ribbon to hold its shape when made into a bow.

To make a handy string dispenser, make a hole in the lid of an empty margarine tub. Put the string in the tub and poke the string through the hole.

If you have **to mail a gift,** protect the bow from being crushed by covering it with a plastic berry basket (like the ones strawberries come in).

Admit your mistakes before someone else exaggerates them!

S
H

Old Rubbish into New Treasures

E
S

T

R

I

N

G

YOU KNOW YOU'RE A TIGHTWAD...

...IF YOU HAVE USED A BROOM HANDLE FOR A TENT POLE, A CAR TRAVEL CLOTHES ROD, A YARD SALE ROD, A CURTAIN ROD, AND A TOMATO STAKE ALL IN THE SAME MONTH!!

It is better to know some of the questions than all of the answers.
James Thurber

Save all of your old calendar pictures for future framing–$ store frames are cheap!

Paint long sticks gathered from the woods a bright color and put them in a tall container for decoration (or leave them unpainted for a natural look).

Mount magazine pages onto cardboard, poster board, or construction paper instead of buying posters for your child's room.

A jar makes a great yet unique flower vase. Add a ribbon around the rim or leave it plain.

Create a boxed bed by painting concrete blocks black (or any color) and top with a board. Place a mattress on top of the board for a modern bed look.

Decorate a wall with straw hats. Very cheap at discount or thrift shops.

Mrs. Butterworth's syrup jars make great colonial vases.

Instead of buying an expensive quilt rack, paint or stain a sawhorse.

For a cheap drafting table, cut down one end of a pair of sawhorses equally (for the drafting table incline) and nail the desktop board you have chosen to the sawhorses.

For a bookshelf, use boards inserted into the steps of a ladder (or you can use two ladders) and paint or stain as you wish.

Another bookshelf idea is concrete blocks or bricks with boards placed on top of blocks. Use the block holes for knickknacks or small books.

To revamp an old trunk, table, or box, cut out favorite magazine pictures (such as Victorian, zoo animals, etc.). Glue on and cover with a brushed-on layer of glue and water to preserve.

Wrap a brick with material for a doorstop.

A heavy plastic or steel bucket turned upside down with four or so top holes makes a great umbrella stand.

If we can't do it fast,

Cover your old ottoman with bright sheets or material and wrap a large ribbon around it so the material will gather. You may pin in place.

Cut leftover bathroom wallpaper into 1-inch strips and paste on the blinds in the bathroom. Now the blinds will coordinate with the walls, and you won't need curtains.

Cut eight place mat-size rectangles of leftover kitchen or dining room wallpaper and glue them together so they are reversible. Cover both sides with clear contact paper. Now you have easy-to-clean place mats that match your wallpaper.

Old wooden pop bottle crates are just the right size for spice cans or jars. Cut some of the sections away to allow space for taller bottles. Hang the crate sideways on the wall.

In a small town the only place you have to stand in line is to shake hands with the minister after church on Sunday.

then we won't last!

Buy large baskets with very small handles (or no handles at all), and turn them upside down. Poke a hole in the middle of the bottom of the basket just large enough for the screw on the top of the lamp. A great lampshade!

Enough cannot be said about decorating with kitchen towels. Use the cotton or blends, not terry cloth. Take old towels; they can be worn or full of holes for this project. Braid them together like a pigtail, glue the braid to cardboard ring to make a wreath for your kitchen, or . . .

Use spray adhesive to cover a worn-out desk pad, press a towel on top of it. It is the perfect size! While you are at it, hang the toweling as an accent wall covering between shelves.

For those jars of jellies and pickles you plan to give to friends in holiday gift baskets, cut squares of old kitchen towels and tie with a bright contrasting ribbon to the tops of the jars.

Storage can be created from discarded flats. What are flats? They are the wooden slated platforms or trays you see at construction sites for stacking roofing shingles. These are usually trashed, so smile at that young Adonis at the building site and he'll not only give it to you, but will load it into your car! Hang two, one above the other, on your kitchen wall. From cup hooks, hang pots, pans, potholders, and decorative items.

An old screen door mounted on the front of an equally high shelf unit makes a super storage cabinet. Looks great in the kitchen with mixing bowls, dishes, dish towels, and napkins on the shelves.

Fool the eye with a folding screen that establishes an entryway in a walk-right-in room. Make the screen out of three old hollow-core doors hinged together, or use several old window shutters. Paint, stencil, or wallpaper to match your decor.

A wallpapering tray, the one that holds water, makes an inexpensive but good-looking indoor garden. Set small pots of herbs in it for year-round use in the kitchen. Or you can fill it with small pots of ivy, small ferns, etc.

Those beautiful pictures of flowers that you see in the seed catalogs can be cut out and glued to a metal watering can. Coat the cutouts, once they are on the can, with a spray sealer. Put a 36"-square of gingham cloth in the middle of your kitchen table and set the watering can on the cloth. Presto! You've got a charming centerpiece.

Antique doorknobs that you find at flea markets, garage sales, and junk shops make attractive tiny vases for a few flowers. Turn them upside down, remove the post and you have the perfect vase for a tiny flower arrangement. Several of these "little vases" look great grouped together.

generates an income of its own.

Your child's old retainer case or empty cassette holder is great to put in your purse for odds and ends such as pills, safety pins, etc.

A pillowcase makes a great toddler costume. (Cut out holes for head and arms and add accessories for a bride, princess, Darth Vader, etc.)

Cut out the foot of an old sock and use as a bandage to hold an ice pack for an injury or to hold a bandage in place.

An old tackle box makes a great sewing box, knickknack box, etc. Paint it! Add decals or cut out a design or flower from contact paper.

Take old rake or broom handles that you may find in other people's trash. You can use them as stakes for your garden. You may paint some red for tomatoes, green for lettuce, yellow for squash.

Don't throw out an ugly wreath. Save and cut sprigs from it for Christmas packages or Christmas scenes.

Squashed or old bows can be refurbished by shredding the ribbons. Cut from outside to center in small sits or cut all the way and use your scissors to curl.

Save all old folders, notebooks, and index tabs to reuse for reports, school projects, gift tags, etc.

It's not how much you make,

If you have a mountain to climb, waiting won't make it smaller.

u *s*

Wrap coffee cans in the appropriate holiday wrapping and put treats inside for guests or for family use.

Baby food jars make perfect gifts with treats inside and a swatch of material over the lid with a rubber band and ribbon and tags.

Don't throw away old Kleenex boxes or trash bag boxes with the hole in the top. Stuff your plastic grocery bags in these and use as a pop-up dispenser!

Save extra garbage bag ties to use for wire jobs—just peel off the paper.

Save your macaroni and cheese boxes, shoe boxes, detergent boxes, etc. Cover in contact paper or material, and use as building blocks for your children. The more, the better, and the more varied in size, the better!

Scope or Listerine tops (large-size bottles) make great votive candle holders (you may want to put a little foil inside).

it's how much you keep!

When we fold our hands in prayer, God opens His.

Us

The tops of your yogurt containers or butter tubs are great "wheels" for a wagon you can make from a shoe box and a shoestring. Put on with brads.

The cola cardboard bottle holders are great as car totes to fill with crayons, small tablets, mini-cars, etc.

The long boxes that hold little bags of chips are perfect for your photo envelopes—scoot under a bed!

SHOESTRING

Entertaining and Exchanges

YOU KNOW YOU'RE A TIGHTWAD...

...IF YOUR IDEA OF AN ANTIQUE IS YOUR ELVIS ON VELVET.

your husband's bringing his co-workers over for drinks and snackies. Don't panic.

For drinks, remove the peel from an orange, lime, or lemon in one long curling length with a vegetable peeler. Add the peel to a glass pitcher of iced tea.

Cut a strawberry or slices of peeled kiwifruit. Don't cut the slice all the way through, just cut to about the middle of the fruit and perch it on the rims of glasses.

A tablespoon or two of grenadine syrup or raspberry syrup added to a glass of orange juice will a create a lovely sunrise effect.

Cut thin slices of orange, lemon, or lime, poke the peel with clove studs, and float the slices in your bowl of punch.

Use cinnamon sticks to stir steaming mugs of hot chocolate, hot tea, or hot apple cider. Yummy!

Use fruit juice to make an **ice ring** for your punch bowl. It looks nice and it won't water down the punch as it melts.

If it weren't for the last minute, a lot of things wouldn't get done.
us

On one of those rare occasions when you and your special other are alone, make a banana daiquiri without the "hard stuff." Whirl a cut-up ripe banana, 2 tbsp. frozen pineapple juice concentrate, and 1 tsp. fresh lemon or lime juice in a blender. Add 1 cup crushed ice, a little at a time. Whirl until it's thick and smooth. Serve right now! Serves 2.

If you are "watering" a crowd, serve punches, they're cheaper than soft drinks or a full bar.

For a tray of cheese, don't waste time cutting up your cheese into silly miniature cubes. Leave it in bricks, wedges, or rounds. Line the tray with leaf lettuce before putting the cheese on, along with a cheese knife or spreader.

To add eye appeal to your cheese tray, add a bunch of grapes, strawberries, or apple wedges.

For a large party, arrange two or three separate cheese trays. Put out one to start, and when that's devoured, call in the reserves.

let's set the table!

If you have a pretty table, let it show. Use place mats instead of a tablecloth, which is really a sheet. If you don't have enough place mats you can make them by cutting fabric into rectangles and ironing a hem under with fusible web.

If we have to sew it,

If you don't have enough matching dishes for a large group, mix and match. Use what you've got and tie in everything with matching napkins.

Dress your napkins up by tying each with a simple **RIBBON.**

Use paper napkins and fold them into *accordion fans.*

Use **unusual serving dishes.** Put sauces, stand-up pickles, or pepper strips in a mug and tie a bow on its handle.

Use a shiny metal colander to hold small loaves of bread or bread sticks.

Garnish your main dish, usually your meat, with cherry tomatoes or sliced red peppers. Poke a few sprigs of fresh dill or parsley around them.

Flowers floating in a glass bowl is an easy-to-make **centerpiece**.

Use lots of *candles* in all different sizes in all different types of holders for your table. If you didn't get a chance to dust, candlelight can be very flattering!

To decorate the rim of a large serving platter, spray it with nonstick cooking spray, then sprinkle on **curry powder or paprika** or chopped dill.

we'd rather throw it!

Fresh herbs tied together with garden twine, ribbon, or raffia are an easy and romantic way to dress up a place setting. Set the little bouquets at each place, or tie them around the napkins with a ribbon and bow.

Put a few sprigs of fresh sage, thyme, or rosemary around roasts, hams, or sliced meats.

Serve stuffing and vegetables inside tiny hollowed-out pumpkins for an **autumn dinner**.

Flowers are too expensive to buy. Make a centerpiece of colorful fruits and vegetables. You have to throw the flowers out, but you can eat your fruits and vegetables later.

Create a **COUNTRY LOOK** for your table by using a patchwork quilt or rag rug as your tablecloth.

Put your bread in thrift store baskets; scalloped seashells and mismatched dishes for salsas or relishes, bright mixing bowls as serving dishes.

Wrap forks, knives, and spoons in individual napkins, and tie with a ribbon or a twist of ivy or honeysuckle vine.

Raid the woodpile and cut some chunks of firewood into different-sized pieces, drill a hole for a candle, and presto! **Instant candlesticks!**

Writing down what you buy

*If you think you can, you can.
And if you think you can't,
you're right.* Mary Kay Ash

Stack miniature pumpkins in a pyramid and glue them together, or use long nails to "staple" them together. Poke colored leaves in between the pumpkins and you've got a great centerpiece!

Gather pine cones, spray-paint them fall colors, and fill an old basket with them. Tie a raffia bow on the handle. Another centerpiece!

Do leaf imprints on your tablecloth. Collect green leaves, paint them on the bumpy side with fabric paint, then press onto the tablecloth.

Cut leaf shapes from bright-colored fabric or felt and appliqué the hem on your tablecloth with fusible web. A scattering of these down the middle of the cloth is especially attractive.

If you want to **get fancy,** fill small clay pots with crumpled-up newspapers about three-quarters full, then mound moss up to about $1^{1}/_{2}''$ over the top rim of the pot. Tie a pretty ribbon around the pot (lavender looks great with the dark green moss). Write your guests' names on small cards and tuck them into the moss.

will shock you to the sky!

Fold a square napkin in accordion pleats, then fold the entire napkin in half. Tie gold or silver cord around the middle in a decorative knot, opening the ends into a fan. Set the napkins on the plates, with the fan end toward the center of the table.

For a table decoration that is **ELEGANT** in its **simplicity,** lay fresh evergreens in a long spray down the middle of your table and tie a ribbon around the center in a simple bow. Evergreens with the little berries look great in this simple arrangement.

Champagne is too expensive! If you're having a home wedding, try serving sparkling cider or sparking grape juice in champagne goblets.

A great centerpiece for that **do-it-yourself wedding** is a wedding cake made out of tissue or papier-mâché—covered foam discs. Frost it with silk cords and rosebuds, top it with a miniature bride and groom. This makes a great centerpiece for a bridal shower or at the reception's guest registration table.

A great way to save money for your wedding is to use silk floral arrangements instead of the real, expensive thing. The silk bouquets can be made in advance with no worry about wilting. Best of all, they can be saved as mementos. The bride and groom can display them in their own home for years to come—a beautiful reminder of their special day.

Beware of small expenses;

Chains do not hold a marriage together. It is threads, hundreds of tiny threads, which sew people together through the years.
Simone Signoret

A beautiful table treatment, the one that holds the real cake, is simply to drape a table with a white sheet to the floor and then swag tulle (that's netting, like the bride's veil) around the table. Gather the tulle at different intervals with big white or silver bows. From the back, pin the bows to the tablecloth. Scatter strings of pearls or other sparkling baubles on the table; weave them around serving dishes, the centerpiece, etc. (Remember to visit your thrift stores for those baubles!)

before we move on to our favorite subject, entertaining for children, here are a few basic tips to make grown-ups' entertaining easier.

Be realistic about the menu of your get-together.
Don't choose recipes that are too elaborate or require last-minute prep. If you only have time to cook one really blowout dish, make it dessert since that's the last impression everyone will take home with them.

a small leak can sink a big ship!

Don't be shy about using ready-prepared foods.
Put a store-bought appetizer on your finest plate, garnish it with
herbs or parsley, and no one will be the wiser.

Do as much work in advance as you can. Bake and
freeze in microwavable containers. Baked lasagna or ziti freezes
beautifully. Pop it in the microwave, add as companions a big tossed
salad and hot French bread, and you have a relatively simple meal to
make and a delicious one to serve.

Or instead of cooking a full meal, serve a variety of snacks like inexpensive finger sandwiches, crackers and cheese, or bite-size pizzas.

for parties kids will remember . . .

Decorations should be bright and colorful. Hang them
from the ceiling and put them on the walls. Rub balloons against your
clothing for a minute to create static electricity, then put them against
the wall and they will stay there!

A great party for outdoors is a "carnival party." What's a
carnival without booths! One way to make a booth is to put a broom
or mop handle between two chairs or cardboard cartons. Hang a
sheet, crepe paper, or decorated cardboard sign on the handle.

Another way to make a booth is with a card table, or you can use a
large cardboard carton or cartons taped together. These booths will
give counter space. Decorate the booths with signs, balloons, and
crepe paper streamers.

Every little bit helps;

What are you going to use these booths for? Lots and lots of fun!

Clown makeup booth. Here's what you will need: water-soluble makeup in red, white, and black, lipstick, rouge, eyebrow pencils and makeup crayons. Any add-ons like noses, glasses, or mustaches and an old shirt to wear while putting makeup on.

Tip: Before putting makeup on that little up-turned face, cover it with a thin coat of cold cream. The makeup not only will be easier to apply but easier to take off.

Here's another booth idea: popcorn! Pop your corn ahead of time and put it in paper bags or cups and let the kids help themselves. Put a jar filled with popcorn kernels on your booth's countertop. Count the kernels ahead of time and tape the number of kernels on the bottom of the jar. Let the kids guess the amount by putting their names and guesses in a box. Closest guesser wins a prize!

Here's another neat game. Set up a **penny pitch** game by stacking old plates and cups on your booth's countertop. Have a small prize on each cup or plate. Give each guest the same number of pennies to throw. If a penny lands on a plate or in a cup, the tosser wins the prize. Make sure the tossers stand 3 feet away from the booth; put a line on the ground for them to stand on.

For a **BEANBAG THROW,** stack paper cups on a box or your booth top and let the guests each have three tries to knock down all of the cups. Again, winners get prizes!

a mansion is built one brick at a time.

You can also use the booth to serve the refreshments. Hot dogs and lemonade and, of course, ice cream!

Children need no boats or planes
In order to fly;
Their minds have sails,
Their thoughts have wings
That seek the open sky.
Author Unknown

Monster Party! When the invitations are sent out for this party, ask the guests to come as their favorite monster: a vampire, a werewolf, Dracula, Frankenstein, or their own creepy creation! A neat invitation for this party theme is to trace around your own hand on folded colored paper. With a marking pen or crayon, you can add creepy details like purple fingernails or scars. The fold of the paper is where your wrist joins your hand. Write the details of the party inside the "hand."

For decorations, just lie down on a large sheet of brown wrapping paper and have someone trace around you. Cut out the silhouette and paint or color it to look like your favorite monster. Make several of these and hang them on the wall near your party table. **CREEPY!**

Monster menu: Spooketti, bloodred punch or Ghoul-Aid (any red punch), Skull Cakes and of course, I Scream (like double-dutch chocolate).

If we can't do it fast,

The **Skull Cakes** are simply cupcakes with icing and topped with those little tiny skulls you find at the $ store or one of those variety stores with "mart" at the end of their name.

Monster games: Bat Man's Bluff! Blindfold one player, spin him or her around. "It" tries to catch the other players and guesses who is caught. "It" gets only three guesses; if "it" guesses right, the person caught becomes "it" and the game starts all over again.

Pin the fangs on the vampire: Draw and color

a large picture of a vampire. (Maybe our Cousin Con will model for it.) Hang the picture on the wall. Cut out fangs (big pointed teeth), one for each player. Players each get a turn to be blindfolded, spun around, then pin a fang on the picture. The player who comes closest to the vampire's mouth wins the game and a prize!

here is a list of a few more party themes. Let your imagination soar!

Puppet shows, puppet making
A real tea party (a great one for a little girls' birthday party)
A Mexican fiesta
Cartoon characters
Sports
A camping trip or hike
Circus
A magic show
Space
Let's make cookies
Slumber party
Pirates
Robots

then we won't last!

we've talked about entertaining a crowd or a small group, and childrens' parties. Here we've chosen something a little different. It's exchanges between each other. Exchanges can be in the form of gifts, thoughts, or time.

Take your children for a walk in the woods. Take a magnifying glass with you. Let them see up close the wonders of nature. This will be a memory.

Before you leave the woods, gather bright-colored leaves. When you get home, you and the children spread out your leaves on the kitchen table. Make a circle of construction paper to fit around your heads and glue the leaves on it.

If you have some leaves left over, cover them both sides with clear contact paper. Cut around the outsides of the leaves, make a hole at the top, loop string or yarn through, hang in the window, and **enjoy the fall colors** as the sun shines through.

Take the family **apple picking** at a local farm. When you get home have an apple-cooking afternoon. Make applesauce, apple butter, or apple pies!

Visit an old cemetery and take rubbings from unusual gravestones. Better yet, take the oldest member of your family and go *ancestor hunting.*

Being a tightwad

Paper and crayon are the only two things you need to make grave-stone rubbings. Do the rubbing with a silver, copper, or gold crayons.

Make a bird feeder with your children. Did you know birds like cracked corn? Cheap at the feed store!

Have a World Series theme party to watch one of the games. The kids can hawk hot dogs and popcorn and everybody can wear their baseball caps.

a mama's love is so unfailing that sometimes it is taken for granted. So whether it's your mama, grandmother, or a favorite aunt, here are some ways we can all say "I love you."

A treasure box: make one out of an old hatbox, full of the grandchildren's works of art and other keepsakes. Doesn't every grandmother in the world pine for a Santa Claus made out of the cardboard tube from a roll of toilet paper?

Make a date with your special person; it can be something simple like sharing a cup of tea while sitting on the back porch or a bunch of wildflowers tied with a ribbon. Rent *Gone With the Wind* and watch it with her; make lunch for just the two of you and tell her that she is appreciated and loved.

Frame some of the kids' artwork for her to hang on her walls, and you know she will. Every grandmother loves lopsided houses with purple trees around it!

generates an income of its own.

Ask her how to make a cake from scratch, or to teach you to knit or how to plant a flower box.

Make a video of your kids just for her.

Volunteer to help her with a project. Maybe her kitchen needs painting or the basement needs a good clean-out!

Round up the children and **wash her car.**

Ask her to help you trace the family tree. You will be surprised at the stories that come from this exchange. Write them down!

And never let her leave without your saying to her, **"I love you"!**

Wrap her Christmas present in your child's drawings. Glue several drawings together to wrap a big one.

A mother is not a person to lean on but a person to make leaning unnecessary.
Dorothy Canfield Fisher

It's not how much you make,

Save the newspapers from special dates: the births of your children, wedding and graduation days. Given later as gifts, these will be cherished.

To mark a joyous addition to the family tree, celebrate with a live sapling. Many new mothers appreciate the symbolism of a gift that will grow and change just as the child will.

Here is a great way to use receiving blankets after the baby outgrows them. Match the sizes and sew them together in pairs. Add yarn, ribbons, and other embellishments. These make great comforters for children, who, when they are grown, can pass them along to their own children.

Speaking of passing down to the next generations, we sisters took the time several years ago to sit down with our grandmother with a tape recorder. She told us about her grandparents and parents. What the world was like when she was a child. How she met our grandfather, the birth of her children…and what our mama was like when she was a child. That grandmother is gone now, as well as our beloved mama, and that tape is treasured and stained with tears.

okay. Now that we have everybody in tears let's talk about brown paper sacks!

Wrap the children's presents to their grandparents in the paper from **A BROWN SACK.** Before you wrap, have the children put their handprints on the paper. Use poster paint and tell them Santa Claus will know it if they make a mess!

it's how much you keep!

Wrap all your gifts with the old grocery bag paper. You cut it apart first and if the sack has JOE'S SUPERMARKET stamped on it, then turn that to the inside of the present. Tie them up with big red or white gingham bows, or wrap one with twine or jute and on top add a decoration of nuts, pine cones, and a sprig of evergreen. Paste gold stars all over another bag.

Welcome a new neighbor with a gift that's sure to make **A FAST FRIEND.** Decorate a file box and fill it with index cards listing the names of your best neighborhood plumber, baby-sitter, dentist, and more.

This is a good way to use the only mug left from a set. Cut a piece of Styrofoam to fit inside the mug. Glue in place and cover the top of the foam with moss. Insert artificial fruit with leaves into the foam. Poke a plastic plant cardholder into the arrangement. Put a recipe card in the cardholder. This makes a great gift for a bride's kitchen shower, especially if you make it personal by writing one of the family's favorite recipes on the card.

Remove the bottom from a tuna fish can. Bend the can into a triangular shape, rounding the sides and flattening the bottom. Paint the can with acrylic paint. Glue a flat piece of lace around the outside of the can, begin at the base so that the seams are hidden. Center and glue a narrow ribbon on top of the lace. Arrange and glue a **tiny little scene** inside. The theme of the little "scene" can be as varied as any of our holidays.

If we have to sew it,

An empty Band-Aid tin makes a great and sturdy **crayon box.** You can paint the can and decorate it with the child's name.

The old empty Band-Aid tin makes a neat *emergency kit* for your purse. Let's face it, if you have kids, you are going to have emergencies and, of course, they always happen when you are away from home. So fill that tin with a couple of safety pins, some Band-Aids, a needle already threaded (stick the needle in a small cork before you put it in the tin so you won't stab yourself), add a couple of headache powders for yourself.

Cocoa cans, baking powder cans, or any other can with a removable pry-off or screw-top cover, can be converted very easily into useful banks. Turn the can upside down with the lid pressed on tightly. Make a slot 1 $1/2''$ long. Paint and decorate. One of our daughters had a "cocoa" tin bank, painted pink with her name on it, in her sock drawer for years. That daughter is grown now, and **she still uses that little pink can!**

Bet you didn't know there are so many ways to use plain ol' tin cans!

Here's how to make a **BIRD FEEDER** with, what else, a tin can! You need two aluminum pie pans and a coffee can. To allow the birdseed to pour from the coffee can to the bottom pie pan, punch several triangular holes near the bottom of the can. Not on the bottom—on the sides near the bottom of the can. To assemble the "feeder," punch holes in the center of both pie pans and in the bottom center of the coffee can. Put the coffee can between the two pie pans, knot a piece of clothesline rope at the bottom and thread it up through the pie pans and coffee can. One pie pan makes the bottom tray, where the food from the coffee can is served. The other pie tin is inverted on top of the coffee can to form a roof. The roof slides up the rope so that you can refill the feeder can.

> *To obtain maximum attention, it's hard to beat a good big mistake!*
>
> us

On with tin cans! Here's how you can use a tuna fish can. Stuff the can with cotton, mounding it up well over the top to form a rounded pad. Cover the cotton padding with a scrap of material, such as a piece of velvet, and tuck the edges of the fabric down into the can. Glue the fabric to the inside edge of the can. You've made a pincushion! Finish it by wrapping the outside of the can with yarn or jute.

Those little 35mm film cartridges can easily be converted into **salt and pepper shakers.** Use a tiny nail to pierce holes in the covers. Paint them or cover them with contact paper and mark one with an "S" and the other with a "P."

Writing down what you buy

Look for mugs, you know where—**$ STORE**—with a humorous saying or design on them. For the fisherman, a mug with a sailboat; inside the mug, stuff Gummi worms! For the boss, stuff the mug with Pay Day candy bars! For your favorite guy, fill the "I love you" mug with Hershey's Kisses! For the mug marked "for our favorite aunt" fill with lemon sour balls. Fill a soup-size mug with packets of hot chocolate and a plastic baggie of little marshmallows!

A pizza pan and cutter, a jar of pizza sauce: stick it all in a box and give it to a teenager!

One year for our Big Sis's birthday, we gave her, from her era, a hula hoop, a jump rope, chalk (for drawing hopscotch patterns on the sidewalk), a ball and jacks, and a Slinky. She loved it! All from the thrift store or $ store!

Take a child's umbrella and with a waterproof marker, write the child's name. Between every other set of ribs alternate drawings of a heart or flower.

Star-struck sneakers will delight a teen. You know where you are going to get the sneakers. You got it! $ store! While you are there pick up some fabric paint. Paint stars all over the sneakers—in gold, of course—or glue on some shapes cut out of felt or fabric; lace those sneakers with wild gold or plaid ribbon.

Just one 36″ ruler can make a yardstick picture frame. You just cut and glue. Great gift for the teachers that put up with our "darlings."

will shock you to the sky!

Here's a nice gift for Dad from his kids. Using a wooden dress hanger, measure off six equal sections on the side of the hanger and mark them. Glue the flat end of a spool, the kind thread used to be on, over each of the six marks. Hang several of Dad's ties on each spool.

It is possible to own too much. A person with one watch knows what time it is; a person with two watches is never sure.

Us

For those people on your list who say **"I don't want anything,"** and you know they will talk about you if you don't, here are a few suggestions. A loaf of bread from your kitchen wrapped in a checked napkin; a window herb garden; a decorative light switch cover that you have painted yourself; a red candle in a candleholder; a napkin holder, scented drawer liner, wind chimes, a house plant, relaxation tape (Aunt Sarie sure needs this one), holiday hand towels, a set of padded dress hangers...the ideas are there, think of some more.

You can buy **stemmed glasses** at the thrift store for pennies. Fill with potpourri (a dollar per bag at $ stores) and put a small candle set in a metal container in the center for elegant decoration.

Beware of small expenses;

One magnolia blossom floating in a punch bowl will send fragrance through your entire house.

showers? We love 'em! Baby, bridal, whatever the reason. Here's how:

Green strawberry baskets stuffed with tissue and filled with candy or such make excellent gifts and party favors.

Add a sticker to your plain white paper napkins for a party.

Cheap punch: Buy the colored punch in plastic jugs and add vanilla ice cream.

When you need to put two cardboard tables together, use a can where they join at the legs. Large sturdy rubber bands or tape wrapped around the legs will work also.

Cut a piece of white paper and fold it to resemble a trifold diaper. Write the shower information inside. Then fold and fasten with a tiny gold safety pin.

Fold a triangle of white or pastel construction paper in the shape of a diaper, and fasten with a small gold safety pin to attach the tag. If you wish, put a small dab of mustard inside one or several of the "diapers." Guests who draw a dirty diaper win a door prize.

a small leak can sink a big ship!

Tie a white napkin around plastic silverware in a trifold diaper.

Use paper cupcake holders to hold mints, etc.

Make a *corsage* for the mother-to-be from fancy baby socks, colorful ribbons, and silk flowers.

Fill several **decorated plastic baby bottles** with jelly beans, candies, bath crystals, or bath beads in pretty colors.

Apply **TEDDY BEAR STICKERS** to a center-piece vase. Place little stuffed bears (from the dime store or toy department) here and there on the table.

If you have a real or toy cradle (or bassinet or carriage), decorate it with ribbons and balloons. Then use it to hold the gifts before they are opened.

Stick self-adhesive bows around outer edge of paper plate. When entire plate is covered with bows, it resembles a *bride's bouquet.*

Spray almost any household throwaway with gold or silver paint to create a decorative item: jars, cut-off plastic bottles, egg cartons, etc.

Make a **shower corsage** from ribbon and netting. Instead of using flowers, fasten small kitchen items to it.

To embellish glass stems, a cake knife, and flower arrangements, tie on lace and flowers.

Every little bit helps;

Give a recipe and grocery shower: A young bride starting married life on a limited income will really appreciate this theme. Not only do guests bring one of their favorite recipes, they also help stock her cupboards for the months ahead.

All of the bridal and bridesmaids' accessories worn are important in perfecting the look, but they should not compete for attention. Often simple, less expensive accessories will look as good as or better than elaborate items.

Beaded wreath shapes are also available and come in different widths. They can be worn as purchased or decorated with additional floral or ribbon trim.

Narrow *satin ribbons* and *simple bows* can add color to your wedding or shower to create a more elaborate embellishment for little money.

Lace ribbon is available in a variety of widths; lace ribbon streamers and wrappings can add a delicate touch.

Look for wedding-oriented accessories at surprisingly low costs (doves, bells, etc.).

Pearl strands are attractive as part of floral sprays and garlands, used as loops and streamers with ribbon accents.

Floral leaves in silver, gold, or green: Use silk or metallic leaves from floral- or craft-supply stores to further embellish your rosettes; just use baby's breath for simple elegance.

a mansion is built one brick at a time.

be kind to your parents. Have a modest-cost wedding. It can be done, one penny-pinching step at a time.

Flowers can drive the price of the wedding up faster than any other item. Use more greenery, candles, and ribbon and fewer flowers in the arrangements to save money.

Choose a wedding date that is close to a holiday to make use of decoration already in place at the setting, such as poinsettias and trimmed trees during the Christmas holidays.

Drape lots of netting to fill in big spaces on archways, doorways, table edges, or wrapped around candle stands.

For fancier invitations, tie on or glue a little bow.

Instead of a bouquet, the bride may choose to carry a family Bible with a fresh flower and ribbon streamers or a rosary, a fan with a small floral arrangement attached, or a simple spray.

Instead of bouquets, bridesmaids may carry floral arrangements in baskets or one rose tied with a ribbon.

Today the custom of having an aisle runner is not necessary, even for the most formal wedding, so *save* the extra expense.

Add a romantic touch to any wedding or reception with simple **heart-shaped decorations.**

If we can't do it fast,

Add special touches to pew bows, using one of the following ideas:
- Tie on smaller bows of contrasting colors or wire other ribbons to the larger bow.
- Tape or glue sprigs of baby's breath, fresh flowers, or silk floral sprays to the bows.

Using crystal or silver or gold is elegant. Doesn't even have to be "real"; buy the fake at a party store.

Balloons are an economical and festive reception decoration, too, and can be a good alternative to elaborate floral arrangements.

Colored potpourri, tiny rings, or confetti can be sprinkled down the centers of reception tables.

There's no need to purchase an expensive guest registry set. Simply decorate a pen by wrapping on floral sprays, beading loops, and ribbon bows with white floral tape. Attach it to a pen holder with a white satin ribbon.

Personalize a plain white *guest book* by wrapping wide, beaded bridal lace or Battenberg lace around the front cover and gluing it on.

For a **wedding reception,** consider using a bright print or floral fabric, a solid-colored plastic tablecloth in one of the wedding colors, or a colored sheet under a lace tablecloth or white netting.

For a draped effect, tie up the corners of the tablecloth overhang, pinning large bows of the wedding colors over the gathered areas.

then we won't last!

One inexpensive idea is to use mirror tiles as a centerpiece base to reflect the color and glitter of the other table decorations.

Use small floral arrangements and votive candles with ribbon bows.

Add color to a candleholder or bud vase by wrapping fabric around the base. Wrap the fabric and gather loosely around the base of the candleholder or vase, securing it with a colored rubber band matching the fabric. Tie several strands of $1/8''$-wide satin ribbon over the rubber band.

Buffet service is the bargain among food service choices. Remember, it isn't necessary to have tables and chairs for each guest, but do have some for the older people attending.

For added embellishment of the **w e d d i n g   c a k e,** drape netting, lace, or satin fabric on the table under the cake.

Purchase one small decorated layer cake and serve decorated sheet cakes.

Decorate a simple cake with flowers or floral sprays, either fresh or silk.

Flowers may be used with, or in place of, a cake top or to decorate the entire cake.

Some shops will not charge for the groom's rental if several other outfits are rented from them. Be sure to inquire.

This is a basic decorator bow: For a bow approximately 8″ across, use 3 yards of ribbon. Measure a tail of about 14″ and squeeze the ribbon together at that point. Make a loop on one side using 8″ to 9″ of ribbon with the right side out, twist the ribbon in the center, and repeat for the opposite side. Continuing to hold the bow in the center, make slightly smaller loops on top of the first ones, until you have four on each side. Be sure to continue twisting so that the right side of the ribbon is always to the outside. Finish the bow by making a center loop, thread a wire through it, and twist tightly to secure the center. Adjust the loops attractively on both sides and trim the tails diagonally or into inverted V's.

For an *oversize version* of the basic bow, for use as pew bows and with larger floral decorations, add an extra set of ribbon "tails."

Got a reason to celebrate? Hang curly colored ribbon from the light fixture over your table. Tie small balloons to the ends of the ribbons at different levels.

Set white votive candles in a clear glass bowl of coarse salt—the kind you put in the ice-cream freezer or sprinkle on ice on the sidewalk—to make an inexpensive **"candles in the snow"** centerpiece.

Create a quick, elegant centerpiece by grouping several votive candles on a 12″-square mirror. Entwine ivy, real or fake, around the bases of the candles.

START A PARTY IDEA FILE. Save magazine clippings of decorations, table centerpieces, and recipes. A photo album generates an income of its own.

makes a good file, the plastic page covers keep clippings clean and neat.

To make an attractive serving bowl, nestle a bowl inside a larger bowl or basket. Fill the space between the containers with parsley, ivy, or fresh flowers. Use the bowl as a serving dish for salads or fruit.

look to nature for some of the best materials to make decorations for your table. Best of all they are **FREE!**

Pine cones can be easily bleached by soaking in a solution of equal parts of liquid bleach and water. Put the bleached cones in a basket and tie a plaid ribbon on the handle of the basket.

Here's another one with pine cones. Paint cones with gold paint and put in a white basket, add sprigs of evergreen among the pine cones and tie the basket handle with a dark green ribbon.

Apples, with the core removed, make great candleholders. Put a candle in the apple, put different lengths of candles in several apples, arrange pine cones, evergreen sprigs, or, for autumn, leaves around the base of the apples.

Always keep a supply of small pine cones—natural or painted—for decorating gift packages.

It's not how much you make,

speaking of gifts—we love them! Giving them, that is. Here's how to make each gift special.

For cheap package decoration, you cannot go wrong with the ribbon that you can curl. Store-bought bows are expensive.

Wrap Christmas papers in white butcher paper or brown mailing paper and tie with raffia.

Going to a party this winter where there is a fireplace? Buy a **bundle of firewood** and tie with a large red ribbon or bow for the hostess.

Make your own Christmas labels. Stick a Christmas tree or other holiday pictures onto a plain white label.

Use Styrofoam trays for gifts with treats—wrap in colored plastic and add a bow and a homemade tag.

Classy wrapping paper for small gifts or gift tags can come from a free book of **wallpaper samples.**

Wallpaper samples make excellent *bookmarks.*

Free newspapers from your local newspaper office make great packaging for shipping or storage or wrapping.

Need a gift to lift someone's spirits? Buy her favorite fingernail polish and tie a pretty ribbon around the top. Add a tag of encouraging words.

A good beach souvenir is a jar filled with sand and shells. Decorate the top of the lid. **A gift straight from the ocean!**

Photo *blowups* that can be done cheaply at discount stores make great gifts. A frame can be bought from fifty cents to a dollar; a special gift.

If you've already splurged on a video camera, put it to work! Video-tape candid shots at a wedding or birthday or reunion and give the tape as your gift.

Good on the **computer**? See a poem you like? Type it on the computer, add your graphics, etc., and print out on paper that matches the decor in your recipient's home. Frame and give as a special gift.

A small, inexpensive **ADDRESS BOOK** is the perfect gift for a student going away to college. Be sure to fill the book with the addresses and phone numbers he or she will need. Add some stationery, stamps, etc.

A gift of paper, pens, and stamped envelopes is a good one for someone who is going away to college or moving.

Embroider a special cross-stitch that you like and keep it in the wooden hoop. Glue lace around the hoop and you have a framed gift or something special for your house.

If we have to sew it,

If you have the Bible tapes, record these for special gifts at Christmas. Also any fairy tales, etc.

Wrap a household shower gift with a kitchen towel. A **scouring pad** can be the bow.

Wrinkled paper can be revived by spraying the wrong side with spray starch, then ironing with a warm iron.

Use the free gift tags in the more popular magazines at holiday times.

Use gift paper around a potted plant. Wrap a ribbon around it.

Wrap a gift for a child with *comic strips.*

Use stickers to decorate kids' gifts.

Shred used gift tissue paper by tearing or cutting into long strips— save that tissue from the last gift you received.

Keep a box of gift-wrapping items: anything you possibly can use from those gifts you receive. Recycle tags, ribbons, flowers, paper.

If you receive one of these gift tags that open like little books, cut and save the front to use again.

Wrap a **TEENAGER'S GIFT** with the newspaper sports page or the fashion page.

we'd rather throw it!

Reuse last year's ribbons by running them through the curling iron.

Buy white paper bags instead of brown bags for all-occasion gift saving.

You can also stamp the bag with a rubber stamp or stickers to custom-make your birthday wish.

Add ribbon or a flower from a hat for decoration on a gift.

Buy or bake a **large batch of cookies** and divide into baggies (that fold over) and tie with ribbon. Add a homemade tag (from your old cards) for excellent favors or thank-yous or Christmas gifts for the neighbors.

Save jars and fill with Epsom salts, food coloring, and a tablespoon of oil for bath salt. Drape lid with material and ribbon for your bathroom or a gift.

Wrap boxes with holiday wrap and ribbons and put "packages" on the wall for holiday grouping or group on the floor in a corner.

When buying gift wrap, get *all-occasion print.* For example, red and white dots can be used for Christmas, Valentines, birthdays, and no-occasion.

Use white or brown lunch bags for holiday or any-occasion gift giving. Punch two holes at the top, tie your ribbon or yarn, and use homemade tags. Use shredded tissue paper for the inside packing. Decorate with stickers or stencils or leave plain.

Writing down what you buy

Use cheap **aluminum foil** for a silver-packaged gift.

Save old card fronts and the verses and messages inside the cards for **future tags.**

Wallpaper samples also make good gift tags. Cut and fold in half and write inside. Hole-punch and attach to your gift.

Considerate cheap gift: coupon gift for services from you. Will carpool extra week, will baby-sit, etc.

Wrap a baby shower gift with a baby's blanket and a diaper pin outside. Use a homemade gift tag.

A basket with tissue paper and sample-size things inside is a practical baby or any-occasion gift.

Gift baskets filled with tissue paper or straw and then filled with bath soaps from the $ store, bath oil, reading material, toys, games, sewing items, baby gifts, travel sample gifts, or bubble bath make very good gifts for any occasion.

Popcorn, caramel corn, jams, jellies, granola mixes, breads, and tea mixes make great inexpensive little gifts, in jars with a swatch of material on top and a rubber band around with a ribbon and a tag.

Good **packing material** ideas are Styrofoam, Easter grass, crumpled newspaper, dry cleaning bags, stale popcorn.

will shock you to the sky!

Grocery sacks make great wrapping for UPS or mail packages.

When giving a bakeware gift, consider giving it with *homemade* bread, muffins, etc.

Here's a cute idea for decorating soap for gifts: You need a bar of soap, pictures, and paraffin wax. Cut out pictures, making sure they are a little smaller than the soap. Dampen the soap and smooth the picture or pictures on. Melt some paraffin wax in a shallow container. Dip just the top of the soap into the wax. Let the soap dry after you put the wax on. You can wash many times with the soap and the pictures will stay on.

Here's a good gift idea for a baby shower: Instead of a bow on the package, buy a package of baby washcloths, fold them in a bow shape, and tape to the top of the package. Mothers-to-be will love this. It adds another gift instead of a throwaway.

Turn a photograph album into a recipe file. Take a square of gingham checked material. Cross-stitch your design using the squares from the checks as your guide. Use ribbon for the edges of the cloth and spray adhesive to glue. Inside the album put favorite family recipes. This is a great wedding gift!

The best way to dry summer blossoms to make potpourri is in the trunk of your car. Yep, that's what we said! The heat of the trunk will dry the flowers and the darkness will help retain color. After a week of their being closed up in the trunk, remove petals and store in plastic bags until you are ready to make sachet bags for gift giving.

Beware of small expenses;

When the first boy arrives, give a gift that will also warm the father's heart. This will bring back fond memories for the new father—you know he's just an overgrown little boy anyway. A baseball glove, a slingshot, marbles, or a spinning top are all good selections. And, until the son is old enough to enjoy them, they can be used as handsome decorations on a shelf in his room.

One of our favorite aunts used to send us postcards when she went on a trip. She would write to us on the postcard, then cut it up into puzzle-shaped pieces and mail it to us. The first time we received one of these we thought our goodol' aunt had lost her brain out of her ear. But once we discovered what those little puzzles were about, they became an adventure for us too. And today, as adults, tears come to our eyes when we think about the thoughtfulness behind those little pieces of paper that came to us in the mail.

For those curious people who shake the box, here are a few ideas to fool them! Sidetrack them with a few deceptive *noisemakers:* loose rice, a baby rattle, or pieces of hard candy. Use a box much too big for the item. Or assemble boxes in descending sizes with the gift in the smallest box. Weight the box with a brick. **We love this one!**

Cover a box with tissue or newspaper and write holiday messages with red and green markers.

To make your gift wrapping go faster and smoother, here are few tips to help you **keep your sanity.** Organize a compact gift center on a shelf in a closet, laundry room, or pantry. If possible, locate this area near a table or other flat surface. Mount curtain rods on the in-

a small leak can sink a big ship!

side of the closet door for paper rolls, tape, and rolls of ribbon. To keep track of scissors, attach them by a telephone cord to the door or table. A box or sectioned drawer is great to hold bows, trinkets, gift tags, and other trimmings. Toss into this box or drawer pens, tape, ruler, glue, and string. Happy wrapping!

A collection of little gifts, preferably all homemade, stuffed into a basket is, in our opinion, the best of presents. Here are a few ideas, all with budget in mind. A basket lined with a checked napkin or piece of fabric and filled with a jar of jelly, homemade or bought, a loaf of bread, a bundle of dried herbs held together with a bright ribbon, a bunch of index cards tied with a ribbon to be used as recipe cards, and a box of homemade cookies.

For a birthday celebration for a special friend, pack a basket with an ice-cold jar of lemonade, cheese and crackers or bread, a shiny red apple or fuzzy peach, and cookies or cupcakes. Then go on a picnic, whether it is in your own backyard, the park, or the parking lot, it will be appreciated.

For the gardener on your list, make a basket, line it with fresh moss. Add seed packets tied together with a ribbon, a garden tool or two, and a pair of garden gloves. The tools can be bought at any thrift store or $ store at a very reasonable price. Some discount centers sell seeds left over from the previous year at a dime a pack. **YES, THEY WILL SPROUT!**

SHOESTRING

Secondhand Clothes

YOU KNOW YOU'RE A TIGHTWAD...

... IF YOU'VE EVER BROKEN A LEG
TRYING TO REACH THE BLUE LIGHT.

let's take a look at your closet! When the mistakes in your closet outnumber the rest of your clothes, you are definitely in need of help. It is time to do some serious rethinking about your wardrobe!

With thought and planning, you can build a coordinated wardrobe that will give you more outfits, with fewer purchases, than what is hanging in there now.

Let's get started!

The key to a successful and workable wardrobe is **coordination.** To get to this point, you will need to build your wardrobe around a color scheme. Begin by choosing the two colors in which you look best. The two colors, like peach and brown, should work well together so that the items you add will easily coordinate. This is the way of getting twice as many outfits from the same number of pieces.

Okay, we hear you! How do you know what colors to use to build this wardrobe? Well, if somebody has died and left you a pot of gold, or you've won the lottery or the church bingo, you can have a private color consultation. Get real! Here's a quick and easy way to discover your **PERSONAL COLORATION FOR FREE!**

The determining factor in discovering our "colors" is skin tone. Skin coloration for all people is a combination of three pigments: brown, yellow, and red. We all have some of each pigment. To identify your skin tone, it's best to look at your skin on the wrist and the underside of your forearm, or, best yet, get naked and look at the skin that is in its "pure" color.

Drape an orange towel or piece of fabric over your shoulders and under your chin. Now, do the same with the magenta color. If the magenta color is the most flattering, wear "cool" colors and avoid orange. However, if the orange looks best, wear "warm" colors on the bottom. Most women need to avoid magenta or orange tints. Remember to do this test in natural light, without makeup; and if you have been "partaking of the dye bottle" cover your hair with a towel.

Now you know your colors, lets get back to coordinating your wardrobe.

Take all of your clothes out of your closet, drawers and shelves. Discard all clothes you have not worn in the past two years. If you haven't worn it in two years you know you aren't going to! Put it in the giveaway bag. Now! With each item of clothing ask yourself, "Does this look good on me?" "Is it still in style?" "Is there something I can add to it to make it more fashionable?" **Be brutally critical;** try everything on and make the decision to keep or pitch on the spot.

With the clothes you have left, decide which ones you want to use as a base for your new wardrobe. Remember your colors. You want to form your base on those items that make you look terrific and feel comfortable wearing.

While creating this new wardrobe keep in mind your work and lifestyle requirements.

Maybe as your base item or items, you have decided on that suit you always get compliments on, or that jacket that fits perfectly, or that

Every little bit helps;

blouse that makes your skin look great. Whatever it is, **we are there and ready to build on our base!**

You can't have everything—where would you put it?   Us

MAKE A "TO BUY" LIST. A list to use as a guide-line for your shopping will help you avoid impulse buying. And re-member, just because it's on sale or "such a good price" doesn't mean you have to buy it. That's how you got all those "mismatches" in the first place.

Organize your lists into categories: shoes, tops, sweaters, accessories, etc.

It's best to dress in *separates* when you go on your shopping trip—it will simplify trying on clothes. If you are trying on a blouse you won't have to take a dress off. If you are shopping for a item to match an existing item, either wear it or take it along with you. We often forget the lines of that skirt or jacket, and it's important to view all the pieces together to see if they give the "look" we are trying to achieve.

a mansion is built one brick at a time.

Let's plan our shopping trip. Shopping takes time, a commodity a lot of us are short on; stay at the task as long as you can, but don't shop so long that you get overtired. It will affect wise decision-making.

We don't even have to say this: Wear comfortable shoes that are easy to slip on and off. In other words, don't wear your lace-up-to-your-knee **COMBAT** boots!

While shopping, think *coordination.* Try to create a variety of outfits from three or four pieces.

If you find a blouse, a pair of slacks, or a pair of shoes you look great in, think about buying two. If it really suits you and you can use more than one color of the same style, it's a good buy.

Check the **care tag** on the garments. Can you wash it in Woolite? Or do you have to have it dry-cleaned? Which isn't cheap. One of my sisters bought a beautiful wool cardigan sweater at a garage sale and it cost her more to have it dry-cleaned than she paid for the sweater. Six months later it was in her garage sale!

Remember to stick to your list. **Avoid impulse buying!** You don't want to buy what you really don't need or wear again.

When you go shopping, don't take husbands or the kiddos! Do we really need to explain why? We didn't think so!

If we can't do it fast,

Every job is a self-portrait of the person who did it.
Carolyn Coats

The basic classics are the clothes that have withstood the time-tested middle ground of the fashion world; they are the framework that the new and extreme clothes bounce off of.

Classic clothing is by nature conservative. The secret to wearing classics successfully is to make them your own by combining colors, adding accessories, and paying close to attention to proper fit and construction of the garment.

Consider this classic. **FROM ONE SUIT,** say, navy blue, you can create the following outfits:

Navy jacket coupled with a **white T-shirt** and pair of khaki pants.

The same navy jacket worn with white **turtleneck** and a pair of great-fitting jeans. A pair of leather mules on your feet.

then we won't last!

The same navy jacket worn with **a khaki skirt,** white shirt with colored sweater vest or a patterned sweater vest, a pair of chunky low-heeled slip-ons on your feet.

The same navy jacket worn with the same white T-shirt and add a pair of white slacks. Wear white hose, add navy-and-white spectator shoes. Add a large red, white, and blue **S C A R F** at the shoulder and neck.

The same navy jacket worn with the same white T-shirt, add a long, flowing printed skirt. On your feet you can now wear those **combat boots!**

The same navy jacket over a nice tailored, classic *shirtwaist dress,* stockings, and on your feet a pair of navy leather low-heeled dress shoes.

The same navy jacket, coupled with its matching skirt, a jewel-neck-line shell under the jacket, **a string of pearls,** a brown or taupe leather shoulder bag, and on your feet those same navy leather low-heeled dress shoes. Drape a paisley scarf over your shoulder. Maybe a little navy, brown, or taupe in the scarf?

The sweater sets are back! You can find the originals at the thrift stores. Wear your navy suit skirt with a soft pink or yellow one. Add a string of pearls and gold chain around the neck, light natural stockings with those navy leather low-heeled dress shoes or taupe leather low-heeled dress shoes on your feet.

Wear with your navy suit skirt a ribbed turtleneck in a medium shade of brown, on your legs, matching leggings in the same shade of brown, on your feet those chunky brown leather shoes.

Wear with your navy suit skirt a long (the length of your skirt) sweater vest. Wear a silky long-sleeved blouse under the vest. How about a nice **STRIPE?** Wear navy stockings and those chunky brown leather shoes on your feet. For the extra touch, add a man's necktie to the blouse!

Do you realize that is ten outfits from the foundation of one suit?

How can you *afford* to buy these clothes?

Resale and consignment stores.

Thrift shops, charity bazaars, church rummage sales.

Flea markets and garage sales.

The wonderful glories of secondhand shopping!

In the first place, you will get lower prices on all your wardrobe needs, including designer and better labels.

The fact is that most of the clothes you find in resale stores or consignment shops are thoroughly washed and cleaned before they are put out on display.

generates an income of its own.

Thrift stores or used-clothing stores do not clean the clothes donated to them. But you can do that! They are cheaper because there is no overhead or many shopping amenities. We've been shopping in these types of stores for years, and while we may have gotten a few germs, we have not to date come down with any diseases. Matter of fact, the thrill of wading through the racks on the chance of finding a real "diamond" is pure contentment and an anticipated **thrill!**

If your daughter has a fancy dance or prom to go to, the absolutely best place to find a dress for her is at a consignment shop near an upper-class neighborhood. Most of the dresses in these shops are like new, worn, in most cases, one time. Remember to **HAGGLE** over the price. To us this is the fun part of secondhand buying. In most cases the owner of the shop will get on the phone with the owner of the garment and nine times out of ten your price will be met!

Okay, you've got the dress! Here are a few ideas for the accessories to go with that dress.

Tie a ribbon at the throat "à la Scarlett" or thread it with a charm from your jewelry box. The cost? In the words of Uncle Ed, "dirt cheap."

With a bare-shoulder dress nothing looks more elegant than a single-strand choker of medium-size pearls. You know by now where you would get those!

While we are on the subject of pearls, there is no one piece of jewelry more classy than a string of pearls. Think of every bride you've ever seen, or the beautiful Grace Kelly or Audrey Hepburn. The elegance

It's not how much you make,

of pearls is enduring, from a long strand to classic chokers. Accent sweater sets, dresses, or even jeans and a T-shirt with a single strand and add pearl earrings. You can even mix pearls with silver or gold jewelry!

There is nothing so plentiful in a thrift store than scarves. Wear a colorful one for a fast "face-lift." Be sure to cue it to your skin tone: warm pink, coral, or peach, or a soft fuchsia, slate blue, or a rich burgundy.

It's a funny thing about life: If you refuse to accept anything but the best, you very often get it.
W. Somerset Maugham

Tie a colorful scarf at your waist instead of using a belt.

Team satin with denim, silk with suede, stripes with checks.

Top a frilly shirt with a man's necktie.

Never mind what "they" are showing this year—the military look, the Edwardian look, the perfectly coordinated ensembles. Don't feel you have to duplicate any one style. Take that part of the look that appeals to **YOU!**

it's how much you keep!

Nothing beats a good old blazer. If yours is getting so old that it is boring, sew jumbo rickrack all around the edges (a glue gun will work as well). Plant iron-on flower appliqués anywhere you like on your blazer. This is a fast-and-fun remedy! For a Chanel look, sew assorted buttons to lapels (match the color, but vary the size of the buttons), edge the sleeve ends and the edge of the pocket with gingham ribbon. You can also add a bow: a long length of ribbon drawn through the buttonhole and tied around the button!

If you haven't discovered that you can wear *menswear,* you've missed out on a whole new ball game for your wardrobe!

Tuck a man's shirt into a skirt or pants or knot one at the waist. Belt an oversize shirt low on the hips or add a large scarf to wrap (your fanny) over slim jeans or a long straight skirt. Be sure to wear a teddy, leotard, or a lacy camisole under the shirt; open a few buttons to reveal the feminine side.

Knot a man's T-shirt at the waist, or belt or sash it at the hipline. Wear your guy's T-shirt as a swimsuit cover-up or a nightshirt or as a miniskirt over leotards. Please make sure the T-shirt is plain, we think the effect would definitely be spoiled if that T said "BUBBA'S TRUCK STOP" or HARRY'S HARLEYS!

Don't forget men's **neckties.** They can be worn as a necktie with your smart suit or a sash around your waist. Add a man's vest over a white T-shirt, a great look with skinny jeans!

If we have to sew it,

Here's one we forgot to mention about jewelry! Check your hardware store out for **skinny chains.** They make perfect pendants when you slip on an old clip earring from the odds and ends of your jewelry box. Or you can just plain old tie some knots in that chain. Just don't come to us for knot removal—that is in the same category as ironing and washing windows.

Sometimes an elegant earring can be used as a shoeclip or a pin for an attendant or mother.

Shoes, especially those with fabric uppers, can be easily embellished for a **one-of-a-kind** bridal accessory. Simply use a glue gun to apply lace motifs matching the dress, or beading or small floral pieces.

Some brides really *break with tradition* and wear a short white dress down the aisle. They add a "train" of veiling at their waist.

The bride's mother and attendants can also save money if they choose a solid-color dressy dress, embellished, perhaps, with rhinestone, pearls, etc.

Don't be shy about adding little flowers, etc., to dress up shoes.

Save money by easily making a **petticoat.** Simply add ruffled rows of inexpensive stiff netting to a purchased half-slip.

Some brides on a really tight budget select a lacy and heavily embellished white top to wear with a full skirt of white veil or silk. The top can be worn again at elegant occasions.

we'd rather throw it!

Types of headpieces available include a cap, wreath or ring, headband, crown or tiara, hat, bow, or floral spray. Add veiling to a white silk bow, a hat, a tiara, or even a headband. Cover and embellish with lace pieces, pearls, flowers, etc.

Many headpieces purchased in full-retail bridal shops cost $100 and up—an average of $150 to $300! Because this is an item that will be worn only once, look for less expensive **alternatives.** Check at resale or consignment shops for comparable styles, consider renting one for a fraction of the retail cost, or make one yourself.

Preshaped forms for caps, wreaths, and bands are available in craft and fabric stores to use as the base for a headpiece. These are made from a variety of materials including: buckram—a stiff fabric that will need to be covered; mesh or open-weave—stiffened shapes with holes large enough to weave through $1/4''$-wide ribbon (they can be worn covered or uncovered); satin—a stiffened shape that doesn't need to be covered.

Hats made of stiff net, open-weave, or straw come in various shapes and are also inexpensive. Satin hats are available too. Most hats don't need to be covered but are usually embellished with laces, appliqués, ribbons, and flowers. For additional interest, weave narrow ribbon through open spaces to add color and texture, wrap veiling or ribbon around the crown, or attach a veil.

To shape a headband wreath, use 18-gauge wire, available at craft stores in 18" lengths or by the roll. The wire can be fabric-covered or plain. Form a headpiece using three strands of wire. Then wrap the shape with white floral tape and satin ribbon (if necessary), securing the ends with glue, and decorate as desired.

When *wrapping* with the ribbon, leave long ribbon streamers and braid or knot ribbons.

For the **SIMPLEST** headpiece, hand-sew a large bow and/or floral spray to a comb or barrette. Add your veil.

Make bows from the bridesmaids' dress fabric.

Add a *short veil* to headbands or other headpieces.

Dyed-to-match shoes are no longer a necessary part of the attendants' attire. Many use gold, silver, or white silk for shoe colors.

If you're making the bride's and attendants' dresses or altering or shortening them, use the extra fabric to make **flowers** for the hair or to insert in the bouquet.

Remnants of wedding dress, fabric, lace, or other coordinating fabric can be used to cover the headband-type headpiece.

Make large, **pouffy bows** from veiling by forming figure-8 loops and wrapping the center with white cloth-covered wire. Add a flower.

For a **DOUBLE-LAYER VEIL,** fold the netting in half and then in half again. With the fold at the top, trim to curve the bottom corners.

will shock you to the sky!

Good veiling does not need to be trimmed—even the most expensive veil can be simply cut to size. Trims may be used, however, to coordinate with the dress.

Scatter beads, lace motifs, or flowers on the veiling. Hand-sew them or glue them on using a strong, quick-drying embellishment glue that dries clear.

Don't throw away outdated **silk ties.** Cut the ends from the large end for a suit pocket handkerchief.

Glue old buttons to old hairclips, or use balloons that are tied on, old jewels from Mom's earrings, etc.

Do you need a *pant coat?* Try cutting off an older long-length coat.

Use your maternity tops with a belt or scarf, or tied to the side with a knot.

Long-sleeved shirts too short? Cut the sleeves off and hem. Dry cleaners charge about $2 per sleeve for this service.

Cover your older belts with a scarf.

Cut the sleeves out of outgrown shirts for the **sleeveless look.**

BLEACH jeans for a different look.

Old terry cloth bathrobes make good **beach robes.** Use them as is or cut them off short.

Buy lots of solid white, tan, or black T-shirts for your small children. They match every pair of shorts or jeans that they have in the closet.

A hood cut from an outgrown sweat shirt jacket sewn to your child's coat makes the unhooded hand-me-down coat a hooded coat!

A cut-up afghan cut and tied off makes a **WARM MUFFLER.**

A vest can be made from an old denim shirt. Cut the sleeves out and hem the armholes, or let them fringe or ravel naturally.

Cut off too short jogging pants for a bum-around look for warm weather.

Insert a long shoestring into the jogging pants where the string has come out at the waist.

A *bathing suit* works great as the top of a dance or exercise outfit or vice versa.

Always **cut the buttons** off clothes that have seen their day. Thread them on dental floss. You will thank yourself next time you need buttons for mending.

a small leak can sink a big ship!

Are the drawstrings of your sweat pants always **disappearing?** They will not get lost in the waistband or pull through, if you sew a button on each end of the drawstring.

Need a short formal? Look through the long formals as your last resort. They can be cut off easily.

Tired of that old housecoat? Sew a seam down the middle and you have a perfect gown or lounge outfit.

If you need a coat, buy a classic trench coat that has a removable lining so that you can get more wear out of the coat during the changing seasons. This will also give you a basic **R A I N C O A T** in any season.

Borrow from your man's closet; his bigger shirts and sweaters and vests will work great and add to your outfits with your suits and pants and skirts. You might also find a few ties for that popular tie look.

Cut the top from control-top panty hose for a comfortable girdle every day.

Extend the life of your black shoes by using a **black permanent marker** on scuff marks.

Pocket T-shirts in every color are found at the $ store and can be worn by a boy or a girl, man or woman. Don't forget to wear your pocket T's under your suit jackets.

CUT OFF a T-shirt for the half-T-shirt look that boys and girls like. Cut a fringe at bottom.

The hand-me-down boy clothes that your little girl has inherited can be made into little girl clothes by adding **tied ribbons or girl-ish buttons**. Do this also to plain white socks.

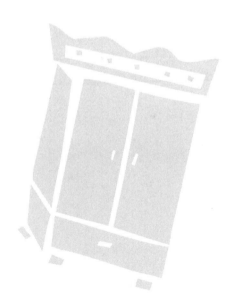

a mansion is built one brick at a time.

SHOESTRING

Tips for Everyday Living

YOU KNOW YOU'RE A TIGHTWAD...

... IF ALL OF YOUR NAPKINS HAVE A
RESTAURANT NAME ON THEM.

"The time has come," the Walrus said,

"To talk of many things:

Of shoes—and ships—and sealing-wax—

Of cabbages—and kings—

And why the sea is boiling hot—

And whether pigs have wings."

Lewis Carroll

we may be halfway through, but we've only just begun! Here you'll find tips to save you time and money in everything you do!

cleaning cheap and quick

Hairspray all over the bathroom mirror? Wipe with rubbing alcohol and a soft cloth.

Remove a stain or mark on the wallpaper with a wadded-up piece of crustless bread and erase away. No kidding, this works! Just don't eat the bread when you are finished.

For getting rid of price tag goo, use a drop of cooking oil on a paper towel.

Someone's gotten chewing gum on the carpet! After you find out who did such a thing and they have been punished for their sin, wrap an ice cube in a piece of plastic wrap and hold it against the gum. After the gum hardens, you'll be able to pull it off.

Here's a test for colorfastness. Bet you can hardly wait! Take a light-colored wet washcloth and rub an inside seam of the garment. If any color rubs off, the garment will run in the wash. Got to hand-wash or spend the bucks and dry-clean instead.

To pretreat ring-around-the-collar, apply a mixture of equal parts water and regular oil-free shampoo. Throw in the washing machine and the rest is history.

We rely on products that cost very little to do our stain removal, laundry, and house cleaning. This is what you need on your shelf: white vinegar, household bleach, ammonia, baking soda, hydrogen peroxide, and a good detergent. You can clean almost anything with these few items.

To remove rust stains in your sink or bathtub, pour hydrogen peroxide on the rust and a sprinkle of cream of tartar. Let sit for 30 minutes, then clean with cloth or sponge. If you have let that rust get really bad, repeat the process.

To keep fireplace ashes from flying all over the room, use a spray bottle of water to slightly dampen ashes before you start sweeping and scooping.

When your energy level drops, use any kind of distraction to keep you on course. Turn on the radio. Set a kitchen timer and say to yourself: "I'll finish this small job before the timer goes off." Take the trash bags out. As you get rid of each bag you will feel liberated from a little more junk. Fix yourself a cool drink and walk outside for a few minutes. Dream about what you are going to do with all that empty, clean space!

Keep narrow-necked vases and other stained glassware sparkling with denture-cleaning tablets. Put one or two tablets, if it is really nasty inside, into the container and fill with water. Wait until tomorrow and rinse clean.

To remove spider webs from the ceiling and corners of a room, put a sock on the end of a broom handle and wipe away.

One part vinegar to two parts water is a great cleaner for all surfaces, such as glass and floors.

Hairspray is perfect for taking ink out of clothes. Spray it liberally on the ink spot and wash garment as usual.

Dingy curtains or clothes can be helped by adding half a cup of electric dishwashing detergent to your regular detergent.

generates an income of its own.

Good ol' baking soda is one of the greatest things ever invented. If you have cats, put baking soda in the bottom of the litter box before you add the litter. Cuts down on the stinky smell only Garfield types have.

Sprinkle a little baking soda inside your rubber gloves. They will slide on and off more easily.

Pour a cup of baking soda and a cup of warm vinegar down the drain to deodorize it. Flush with hot water after waiting 15 or 20 minutes.

Sprinkle baking soda on rugs or carpeting. Freshens nicely. Don't forget to vac up after 15 minutes or so.

Make a paste of water and baking soda and clean the resident artist's crayon marks off the wall.

Sprinkle your car windshield, lights, and chrome with baking soda and scrub gently with a wet sponge to remove bugs and their do.

To remove black heel marks from linoleum and vinyl floors, sprinkle baking soda and wipe clean with a wet sponge.

You can use baby shampoo for fine, delicate washables.

Instead of the expensive detergent for certain fabrics, salt added to the wash keeps colors bright (about 1 tablespoon).

Mix one cup ammonia, 1/2 cup vinegar, and 1/4 cup baking soda together for a cheap, powerful cleaner.

It's not how much you make,

Fill the soft-soap container with cheap liquid dishwashing detergent and make it antibacterial by adding a bit of ammonia or bleach.

Use shampoo on dirty collars. It works!

Teachers do not have to wash chalkboards. Clean them as often as you like with a product like oil soap spray.

Dampen a washcloth with a dab of liquid fabric softener for the same effect of the commercial softener sheets.

Instead of expensive fabric softener, use $1/4$ cup white vinegar in the last rinse of the wash.

Goop hand cleaner and a toothbrush will get almost any stain out of clothes and tennis shoes.

To keep silverware tarnish free and to save on silver cleaners, keep a piece of chalk in a silverware box or cabinet.

A damp, but not wet, broom will help your carpet stay clean if you do not have a vacuum cleaner.

Mix baking soda in with your carpet deodorizer to lengthen its life and save money.

Instead of carpet cleaner, white vinegar mixed with liquid dishwashing detergent and lukewarm water will remove many stains in carpet and furniture.

Instead of brass and copper cleaner, use vinegar on a sponge. Sprinkle sponge with salt and rub. Rinse and dry with a cloth.

When your Brillo pads have run out of soap but still have some life for scrubbing, place a soap chip inside the pad or pour dishwashing liquid on it. Remember to save all pieces of soap, let dry, and store in a plastic bowl for times like these.

For heavily soiled bathrooms, tiles, and windows, mix $1/2$ cup vinegar with 1 pint rubbing alcohol and 1 tbsp. liquid dishwashing detergent with enough water to make a gallon.

Clean the commode by tossing in a denture tablet.

Use window cleaner for patent leather shoes.

When you wash, use cold water whenever possible. Your clothes rinse better and this helps your colored clothes stay brighter and it saves on the hot water bill!

Use kerosene to clean and kill the mildew off the tiles in your bathroom.

An old broom can be revived by soaking it in water and reshaping it the way you want by using rubber bands to structure it and then drying it for a few days.

If you need to wash a necktie, put it in a jar filled with a small amount of detergent and shake. Rinse and dry flat.

If we have to sew it,

An ordinary crayon is a good laundry marker.

The best place to find a helping hand is at the end of your own arm.

To clean your glass windows, add ammonia to the water. Old fashioned cornstarch with $1/4$ cup water is also a good mixture.

Windows also wash better with $1/4$ cup white vinegar in warm water.

Old nylon stockings make great window and car chrome polishers, as well as ties for garden stakes.

To clean painted woodwork stained by grease and smoke, dissolve old-fashioned dry laundry starch in water. Paint it on, and when it's dry, rub with a soft brush or clean cloth. This removes the stains without removing the finish.

Putting stained plastic storage containers outside to dry in the sun removes the stains.

we'd rather throw it!

Put a few bath towels in the washing machine when you wash your shower curtain. The towels, as they rub back and forth against the curtain, remove soap scum.

Put ammonia in an aluminum pie pan and place it in your oven overnight. Wipe down oven with a damp sponge the next morning.

Banish tarnish: Place a piece of aluminum foil, shiny side up, on the bottom of a glass bowl or glass pan. Fill the container with a solution made of boiling water and few teaspoons of baking soda. Soak your silverware; you will know when it's ready, it will be shiny silver!

Remove excess water from shower doors or tile walls with a small rubber squeegee.

The best way to remove soap scum from showers, tubs and the surrounding tile walls is with soap. When you are finished with your shower, while standing there in your birthday suit, rub a bar of soap on your washcloth and wipe down the doors and walls, and rinse. You can get dressed now!

Remove pet hair from upholstery with a damp sponge.

Got of bunch of "single" socks? Put one on each hand and dust your plant leaves.

To remove rust from household tools make a paste of 2 tbsp. salt and 1 tbsp. lemon juice. Apply paste to rusted area with a dry cloth and rub.

new uses for everyday items

A bandanna makes a cute bib.

If there is one thing that will make you forget your religion, it is hunting for the nearly invisible beginning of a roll of tape. Next time after you use the tape, stick a paper clip at the end. Your religion will remain intact and you can tape to your heart's content.

If you have some old lingerie that you do not wear any longer, cut off the lace and decorative embroidery and use it to make small pillows, sachets, or baby pillows. Old slips are especially good for this. Attach a ribbon to the sachets so that they can be hung in closets or on bedposts.

Still have some trim left from the lingerie? Make small squares and fill with sand, your kids won't miss it from their box, for pincushions. Your pins and needles will stay sharp. This is a great idea for diaper pins too.

Use a plastic grocery bag as a disposable pooper scooper for Spot.

will shock you to the sky!

An empty margarine tub or jar or some other small container. These will be put in each box and will be used to hold things like: safety pins, paper clips, buttons, puzzle pieces, game pieces and those hateful little shoes that go to the doll starting with "B."

Place a couple of plastic grocery bags near the back door. When you come in from doing yard work to go to the bathroom or get a drink of water, slip a bag over each shoe to protect your floors from the outdoor grit and grime.

Stick a couple of plastic grocery bags in your purse for wrapping dirty diapers.

To keep junior from sliding around in the high chair, line the seat with a small rubber bath or sink mat. You may have to trim it a little bit.

Put a large soft towel in the bathtub to keep toddler from slipping and sliding.

For smart storage, recycle plastic peanut butter jars to store rice and other grains, beans—any dry goods that should be kept fresh and bug free. Since the jars are see-through, you don't have to label.

Old terry cloth towels should never be thrown away! Cut them up and use them as dishrags or dish-drying towels. Usually the towels we have for our bathroom are thicker

Beware of small expenses;

and more absorbent. And when the terry has finally worn off, still don't throw away. Use as rags for your meanest, dirtiest job. Then you can throw them away!

Cut empty 2-liter plastic soda bottles to a height of 6 inches, then place sacks of flour or sugar in the bottles' bases. This keeps the sacks from toppling over and they are easier to handle.

An old wooden crate stained, natural, or painted makes a great place for boots and messy shoes when coming in the door.

A large basket or huge flowerpot is great for those magazines.

The grasslike carpet or green felt is safe on your porch.

The plastic runners that have "teeth" can be used on porch steps to prevent slipping in rain or snow. Nail (or glue) the cut-to-size pieces to the steps with teeth side up.

Railroad ties make perfect outliners for your patio for dirt, rocks, flower borders, and above-ground gardens. Stack two to three railroad ties on top of each other . . . fill in with dirt.

Sew two napkins together at their edges and fill with a pop-in pillow or stuffing. This is a quick and inexpensive way of making decorative pillows. Shop the thrift stores and garage sales for super-cheap ones.

a small leak can sink a big ship!

Make pretty pillows and matching doilies out of four place mats and napkins. Use the quilted place mats trimmed with lace. Use on tables, seats of straight chairs, or rockers. Make a pillow with matching napkins.

A large plastic lid and an empty spool of thread make a great dollhouse table.

Use your leftover peel-and-stick tiles for cabinet bottoms and doll-houses.

Never buy shelf paper again. Use free wallpaper samples.

Buy inexpensive plastic pencil pouches for travel and organization of cosmetics—much cheaper than makeup bags!

Old round-top clothespins make great "little people" toys; add material and ribbon at neck and put a face on with marker.

Old wire album-stands are great for saving folders, cardboard, notepads, and papers by the phone area.

Find a timber yard, a carpenter, or a shop teacher, and gather the discarded blocks of wood for children. Sand with pieces of sandpaper–all shapes and sizes and they are free! Painting is optional.

Wallpaper stores have discontinued wallpaper sample books free.

Every little bit helps;

Save old school folders to cut up for dividers, school projects, gift tags, picture backings, etc.

Make a car necklace from a shoestring. Tie on a penlight, a rattler, etc., depending on your child's age.

Save your paper bags and Styrofoam containers from fast-food places for your work lunches.

Flat box tops make excellent stack trays for papers. Cut out one end and cover in gift paper or contact paper and use paper clips to stack them together.

Use the Styrofoam egg cartons for drawer organizers or for emergency ice trays.

Recycle your dry-cleaning bags for travel or for plastic trash bags. Tie a knot in one end!

Don't buy expensive teeth-whitening products. Use ¼ tsp. each baking soda and salt mixed in your hand or a container, add enough hydrogen peroxide to make a paste, then brush.

Use the green foam or any Styrofoam to store pierced earrings.

Old maps make great game boards. Old maps with a layer of clear contact paper also make great room decor. With a piece of glass over a map on a table, you have an interesting conversation piece.

a mansion is built one brick at a time.

I want my kids to have all the things I could never afford. Then I want to move in with them.

M & M's make great game tokens.

Cut fronts from old greeting cards and write on the back of the pictures for quick postcards.

Save meat trays for painting or for messy projects. Wash the trays first.

We like the idea of keeping potato chips fresh, but those chip clips are too expensive and too easy to break. Use a rubber band and fold around entire bag of chips from the folded down top to bottom. Or just use a clothespin.

Those huge pickle jars make excellent cookie, pasta storage, cereal, or snack jars.

A baby gate makes a great dog gate too.

If we can't do it fast,

A cut piece of lattice board natural, painted, or stained, also makes a great barrier for a pet.

Fingernail polish makes a great temporary mosquito bite nonitch solution.

Put peanut butter instead of cheese on your mousetraps. Works like a charm!

An empty cassette-tape container makes a great carrier for pins, pills, etc.

Those plastic hold-up things that come in the box of a delivered pizza make great dollhouse tables.

Mesh laundry bags make great bags for the beach for toys. Shake and the sand comes out before you enter your house.

A fan is a great substitute for those expensive noise machines that put people to sleep.

Use large nails for hooks in your shed instead of purchasing expensive hooks. Two nails spaced approximately 4 inches apart hold your rake, shovel, or broom upside down.

Flat saucers make great coasters.

Those old terry cloth drink covers (that kept bottle drinks cold) make neat skirts for Barbie dolls.

then we won't last!

A wading pool is a great sandbox.

The baby's hooded towel converts into a very much used towel for the car when the children are older and have those spill "accidents." Also fits your hand perfectly for a car-drying towel or washing rag.

Visit those used-car-parts stores for the car that lacks an ashtray, a window handle, etc.

A large pillow in a regular basket makes a great pet bed.

We overlook so much happiness because it costs nothing.

Cut up old washcloths for dollhouse washcloths and towels.

A large piece of cardboard or a huge plastic bucket is the greatest sled.

A cardboard visor used inside the car to protect from the sun can be used on the outside of the windshield in bad frost and snowy weather for a cleaner windshield. Be sure to secure it with the windshield wipers.

Newspapers make excellent window-cleaning rags. No streaks.

You can use cookie cutters for furniture stenciling.

A good sturdy box makes a footstool when you're working at your desk or the computer. Cover it.

Those clay flowerpot bottoms are perfect outside patio ashtrays.

A piece of latticework cut in half lengthwise can make a good dog fence outside with several pieces placed around your yard or patio.

Popsicle sticks make great dollhouse shutters.

Those cloth liquor bags make a protective bag for your camera, small tape player, etc.

A dog sweater can be made from a regular sweater by cutting off the sleeves. Cut holes for arms, legs, underside.

Use your child's outgrown sipper cup for hot coffee or other beverages in the car. No need to buy a special cup.

generates an income of its own.

Do not buy a portable desk for your child in the car or for someone sick; use a cookie sheet.

Worn pillowcases (bought for 10 cents or so at yard sales) make great covers for storing clothes. Slit at the top and they're better than nonbreathable plastic!

Oatmeal boxes make excellent drums.

Cut a slit like an X in an empty prescription bottle bottom for a toothbrush holder for traveling.

For an ice pack, use a zipper-lock plastic bag filled with water and keep in freezer.

Decorate a cardboard Coke carton for a garden tote.

Save cardboard from used tablets, new shirt cardboard, etc. to use later for crafts, messy projects, children's drawings, or for a mailing strengthener.

Want to enjoy your vacation a little more? Buy an inexpensive shoe bag on a hanger at the dime store and hook on the back of front seats and fill with fun things as you travel. Also, one can be used for your maps, etc.

Use poster board or recycled cardboard and magazine pictures to create a memory game (shapes, letters, pictures, etc.).

It's not how much you make,

Glue felt to the top of a shoe box and put felt pieces and shapes inside the box for an instant felt board game. Make your own tape of stories for your child to listen to at night or while traveling. (Also works with regular books for adults.)

Save all old squirt bottles for outside water play.

Make dollhouse or puppet people by saving Popsicle sticks and put real-life pictures from magazine and catalogs for faces.

String boxes together with shoestring and tie to tricycle for a long train. Animals and dolls can ride.

Make miniature puzzles from old fun-memory snapshots glued onto cardboard. Cut into puzzle pieces and keep in an envelope with the name on front. Also use magazines or poster pictures.

Use a brown paper bag for a puppet. Use the end crease for a mouth. Add eyes, etc.

Make an obstacle course with old tires. Tires can also be painted.

Just because you're cheap, you don't have to be ungrateful. Make your own thank-you notes by folding paper in half and gluing pictures of an old card on the front.

Use toilet paper tubes for storing extension cords neatly or for extra wires in shops.

it's how much you keep!

Make decorative magazine and file holders out of empty detergent and cereal boxes covered with gift or contact paper.

Use a belt with a lot of holes to hold your toddler in the grocery cart seat.

Use a long spiral phone cord and tie to a belt on your toddler for one of those spiral leashes you see in the mall.

Use the little tops to nonaerosol hairspray pumps for dollhouse wastebaskets.

Use the colored tops to aerosol cans for rubber bands, paper clips, earrings, Q-Tips, etc.

Tie a shoestring to an empty laundry basket for a child's make-believe wagon.

Save the plug-in cords to old appliances and reuse for other appliances. Most of the time they fit.

Cut a hole in an old round laundry basket for a toddler's basketball goal.

Save all used folders, notebooks, and index tabs to reuse for reports, school projects, gift tags, etc.

Use old business cards for flashcards.

If we have to sew it,

Got an older comforter? Convert into a sleeping bag; sew or pin sides.

Use empty butter tubs, whipped cream tubs, etc., for lunch containers.

Getting rid of LPs? Use old album covers for file folders, or for sending photos or breakable items.

Make a dog bed from a laundry basket cut out on one side.

Use Coke can tabs for picture hangers. Glue to back of picture frame with just the top of the clip showing so as to nail easily to wall.

A mesh laundry bag or potato sack are good bathtub toy holders.

Glue cardboard onto four empty sewing spools for a dollhouse bed. Stack more on top in smaller size for banisters. Paint.

Glue a round or square piece of cardboard to an empty sewing spool for a dollhouse table. Paint.

Buy a clear hall runner and cut for car mats. Hall runners have teeth on the underside and will match all colors.

Printing shops throw away odd sizes of paper. Use for cards, arts and crafts projects, children's school projects. Also for bookmarks.

we'd rather throw it!

Checkbook boxes make great drawer dividers.

A short and small looped white shoestring strung with empty plastic spools is great for a baby toy.

Make dollhouse stools by draping a piece of material over an empty spool and place a rubber band over the fabric for a draped look.

Leftover washable wallpaper can be cut into desired sizes for washable place mats.

A bar of soap takes the place of a pin cushion.

A sink plunger marked according to your hem length and moved around the bottom of your skirt functions as a dress hem guide.

Wrap the non-heat-taped water pipes that may be accessible to cold weather with an old flannel-backed tablecloth and put duct tape around it. Do this also to the outside faucet and place a coffee can or small bucket over it. Will save in the long run in keeping those pipes from bursting.

Cover coffee cans with contact paper and use as canisters or to hold other items.

Use a toothpick as an emergency "screw" for your glasses.

Use an old plastic wastebasket for buckets. People throw these away by the thousands!

Writing down what you buy

A small rubber racquet ball can be used as a sink stopper.

Instead of expensive dog dishes, put your pet's water in an angel food cake pan or Bundt pan and place a wooden stake in the center to keep it from being carried off. Put the stake in the ground. Use another one for the pet food.

A good idea for a bird feeder or a birdbath is an angel food cake pan or Bundt pan filled with water and a plastic cup placed in the hole filled with birdseed. Nail or attach at a high level to house or shed or pole.

Mismatched socks can be used for dusting or for car rags (or puppets).

One half of a paper plate can be a dustpan substitute.

One half of a paper plate stapled or glued to a whole paper plate and covered with contact paper makes an excellent napkin, pen, or note holder. Hang on the wall with a soft drink tab glued to back.

Fill nail holes with white toothpaste, or white or colored soap, to match wall. For a colored wall, use color crayons.

Use old irons or bricks for bookends.

Pegboard and golf tees work for a bulletin board.

will shock you to the sky!

Reflective tape in the numbers of your address or letters of your name can personalize your mailbox.

An old bathmat under your rugs is excellent for non-slip purposes.

Pencil eraser is good for cleaning piano keys and other slick surfaces.

Clean your windows with kerosene for a good mosquito repellent.

Reuse manila or mailing envelopes that are large in size to mail other things. Stick a large label on the writing part. Place a label over the old address.

Traveling with a small baby? A rectangular laundry basket makes a great tote that doubles as a little crib for the hotel room. Also a great nap bed when you're visiting someone's house.

Two inexpensive umbrella strollers, taped or belted together, form a double stroller for twins or babies close to each other in age.

Save that outgrown umbrella stroller for your daughter's doll stroller. This holds true for her high chair and walker too.

When the adhesive on an envelope or a stamp fails, try some clear fingernail polish.

Beware of small expenses;

For a small family cookout, use your oven rack or cooler rack over a big kettle pot. Fill the kettle with charcoal.

If you need a chalk holder, use an old lipstick tube.

Use cloth hair-set tape to label freezer items. It sticks and you can write on it.

To repair white appliances, use white typewriter correction fluid over the scratches.

Instead of buying extra ice cube trays, use your egg cartons in a pinch.

Pine needles in the corner of a dog's bed keeps the fleas away.

Old shower curtains, tablecloths, and curtains make great drop cloths.

Do not throw away any cakes of soap. Keep pressing them together to make one giant bar. Use a little water to keep shaping your soap into decorative balls or a regular shape.

An elasticized cord hooked on the sides of your garbage can and over your garbage can lid keeps dogs and other animals from rummaging.

Use modeling clay to keep as a mold for flowers.

a small leak can sink a big ship!

The cardboard bolts on which fabrics are displayed in fabric stores can be made into handy little bulletin boards. Cover one side with polyester batting. Place a piece of fabric or burlap over the batting, pull tightly around the back, and staple in place. Add a hanger at the top of the back and hang in kitchen for notes and coupons or by the phone for a message center.

Here is a hint for that summer picnic table. Try using a laundered shower curtain for a table cover. Because the shower curtain is extra long, it will cover the picnic table fully.

When the shelf-lining paper in your cabinets and drawers wears out, replace it with no-wax self-stick vinyl floor tile. Easy to clean, and you will be a grandmother before it wears out, unless you plan on walking on it.

Make pincushions from scraps of bright fabric fitted tightly over steel wool balls. The steel wool will keep your pins sharp and in their place.

Just one more salt hint. Get rid of weeds or unwanted grass between patio bricks or sidewalks by spreading—you guessed it—salt on them. While you are sprinkling put a little water down on the salt.

Don't throw away leftover popcorn, freeze it. Then sprinkle it outside during snowy days. The birds love it!

After using them in the dryer, save those white fabric softener

Every little bit helps;

sheets that come in one piece. They are a great stabilizer material to use for quilting soft sculpture items instead of batting.

Use an old flour sifter, the kind with a crank you turn, when planting flower or vegetable seeds. It is the perfect spreader to use when a light layer of earth is needed to cover newly planted seeds.

cheap and easy
decorating ideas

The space inside your home should be your own little world. It's where you do what you want, where you can shut out the rest of the universe or, if you choose, invite others in to share your surroundings. Making it your own is easier and cheaper than you think.

If your paint is lumpy or contains some other junk, stretch a pair of panty hose over the top of a clean coffee can and strain the paint. No more excuses, get your brush and get busy.

Copy and enlarge vintage family photographs for instant art. Black-and-white photos, framed and hung on a bright red or yellow wall, are smashing!

If you have small pictures you would like to mount on the wall and would rather not use a nail, glue a piece of Velcro on the back of the picture and a corresponding piece on the wall. Works great!

a mansion is built one brick at a time.

If it's in the middle of winter and you think spring and summer will never come, here are a few illusions to fool yourself: Remove curtains or drapes and hang lacy panels, tie back with a pastel ribbon. Paint wicker furniture and bring indoors; wrap the cushions "present-day style" in bright scarves, fabric remnants. Roll up the carpets or rugs and roll out rattan mats. You can stencil those mats with bright spring borders. Use flowers, ducks, or watermelon slices. Hello spring!

Okay. So it's 105 degrees in the shade and you're dreaming about the first snap of cold, warm fireplaces, and hot chocolate. Here's another "fool yourself." Drape furniture with bold plaid throws, patchwork quilts, or that afghan your aunt made for you. Layer a fake oriental or dark geometric-pattern rug on top of the wall-to-wall carpeting. Cover pillows, again present-day style, with corduroy, flannels, or velvets.

Give oomph to a tiny bedroom with a bold use of color; a crisp blue-and-white comforter cover and shams can be made from sheets, and they don't need to be expensive sheets or new ones. Search your thrift stores and garage sales for the best buys.

Paint can renew an old nightstand. Use a matching color or contrasting color to go with those new blue-and-white shams and comforter you made. To match, paint the nightstand blue or white; to contrast, paint it a shade of dull red or dark yellow. Bring touches of the red or yellow into other parts of the room, with throw pillows on the bed or a (fake) flower arrangement done in the reds or yellows.

If we can't do it fast,

Happiness is found along the way, not at the end of the road.

Put old objects to new uses. Use pitchers as vases, a quilt as a table cover, quilt squares (a find at flea markets) framed and hung on the wall in a grouping. Old vanity doors or shutters can become a window treatment with fabric hung inside their openings with mini-rods. Put a basket on the floor at the end of the bed and fill it with bright balls of yarn that go with your color scheme. Get busy!

Ribbon in decorative patterns makes great borders for room accents (around a mirror, headboard, ceiling or wall border).

Use a small string-mop or a commode mop and paint to swab color on an ugly ceiling or wall.

Don't have a green thumb? Artificial plants are so realistic now, you can use them outside—they look real and are weatherized and are also very inexpensive compared to real plants—and they don't die.

then we won't last!

Make a canopy for a bed with a piece of rectangle fabric and a curtain rod; sheets are great to drape too, perhaps from a hoop bracelet hung on a cup hook from the ceiling.

Ribbons make excellent tiebacks.

The wooden letters of B-A-T-H painted in a coordinating color to your house and mounted on the bathroom door not only look great but let guests know where the bathroom is.

Shower curtain liners are great for shower curtains and much cheaper; they also cover outdoor furniture seat cushions.

Work those jigsaw puzzles and when finished, glue the puzzle onto cardboard for the backing and "spray-gloss" the puzzle (optional) and hang!

Put old junk tools on the wall or around the ceiling for an old-timey look for a den, shop area, or rec room.

A square tablecloth on a rectangle table turned so that the corners are in the middle of the table adds character to your table and shows off the wood on the corners of the table, yet protects the most used table area.

Baskets on the walls and ceilings are a great look.

If you have a footstool that is too hard on your feet, tie a decorative pillow to it with matching ribbons on two sides.

Being a tightwad

Pin a decorative scarf to a regular pillowcase. Use the pillowcase side for sleeping, flip over for a sham look.

A valance cut the length of your bed frame to floor makes a great bed ruffle. Tack or nail the material to the bed, or also sew the valance to an old sheet for the under-the-mattress bed ruffle.

An old quilt can be cut up for window valances, pillows, wall hangings, etc.

Pillowcases folded in half over inexpensive flat foam make the most comfortable and inexpensive way to cushion your chairs.

To get a different look for very little money for a piece of furniture you like, paint the wood; let dry only about 5 minutes and gently wipe with a cloth as much as you want. It will give an antique look.

For that new "old cracked" look on furniture, spread on Elmer's glue heavily and let dry until it cracks.

Paint concrete blocks a bright color and stack with holes in front to organize office supplies, magazines, files. Top the two stacks with a board or door to make a desk.

Use deco paints to paint a window that needs a little character.

Gold-leaf a picture frame: Gather leaves, spray gold, and glue in a design formation around an old frame or mirror.

generates an income of its own.

Cattails and sticks found by the interstate are great for decoration.

Wallpaper can be folded into fans and used as wall decorations.

Sheets make great washable tablecloths. You can add fringe or use a glass top.

To display a quilt on the wall, tack and stretch it over a piece of wood; or drape it over two broom handles to be hung from the top by rolling quilt over it and tacking it, or by using country ribbons sewn to the quilt as loops for the top handle to fit into. You can also purchase the plastic tubing that goes around shower curtain rods to get the right color. The bottom handle is for weight.

Do not buy curtain rods; buy wooden dowel sticks at Wal-Mart stores for about 20 cents. Paint or stain if desired. Use cup hooks to hold the rod up.

For a special award or favorite poem or Bible verse, use the plastic photo frames.

If you have an old pair of floral tier curtains that you're sick of, here's a face-lift that will make you love those old curtains again. Use the old curtains on the bottom half of the window and at the top, add a valance of little gingham checks or small plaids. Don't have any old curtains? Hit those garage sales or thrift stores!

It's not how much you make,

Stuck with an ugly view from one of your windows? Be positive! If the top half of your window gives you a bird's-eye view of the sun and the moon, clouds, and stars, don't rob yourself of such a view but concentrate on shutting out the "uglies" instead. If there's sunlight, mass thick plants on the lower windowsill. If the windowsill is too narrow or there isn't one, add a single shelf across the window. There are dozens of plants that even a brown thumb can't kill. Boston ferns, big and fluffy, ivy, long and trailing, are especially suited for this kind of treatment. And if all else fails, the artificial plants are now so realistic that only by touch can they be distinguished from the real thing. $ stores have these fakes.

An old stained-glass window or panel suspended from hooks and chains that have been mounted either from the ceiling or the window frame will let in rays of soft, colorful light.

Stretch a piece of crochet or a section of lace (cut from an old curtain or tablecloth) between two interlocking frames or across the back of a single nail-pegged frame.

Make a shutter by hinging an old cabinet door to your window. Paint to match or contrast, or stencil a design on the center panel. If there isn't a center panel on your old cabinet door, only a frame, stretch fabric or an old piece of quilt between two spring rods in the opening.

A lace tablecloth makes a great curtain! Garage sales and thrift and dollar stores have the cheapest prices. Sew a pocket or casement at one end of the tablecloth for the rod to go through and hang. What could be easier?

No sewing, just insert the rod through the top hem. Tie back with decorative rope, braid or ribbon. A second sheet of same design can be used in other parts of your room. Drape a table, throw pillows for the couch or cover a bench or old chair.

Two lengths of contrasting fabric (why not use a floral with a small stripe or a plaid with a stripe?) can be twisted together to form this valance: Drape over and under your rod once or twice, depending on the width of your window; tuck the ends behind the back corners of the rod. Add side curtains or drapes. A word to the wise, two and a half or three times the width of your window is the amount of fabric you will need for this treatment.

For a kitchen, bath or child's room, this is the sweetest curtain ever: kitchen towels attached to a rod with clothespins. Paint the pins to match or contrast with the fabric.

If you have a piece of an old lace tablecloth that has at least one good corner, you can make a great looking valance above those tired old tiers. Just cut so that one good corner hangs in the middle of the valance. The cutting line should be 3" longer than width of your window; this is to form the pocket for the rod. Sew or use fusible web for making the pocket. (Note: You will need a double curtain rod to hang both the tiers and the new valance.)

Here's what you can do with an old flower-print tablecloth. Cut off the border and either hem or outline with bias tape. Between each flower "section or square" put in a 4″ dart to add softness to the valance. Sew grosgrain ribbon at each dart, enough to tie in bows around a wooden rod. For a softly tailored valance, cut a strip of fabric about 18″ wide and twice the width of your window. Border bottom of valance with ribbon or bias tape and hem the sides. Then set in box pleats along the

If we have to sew it,

top edge, placing them as close or far apart as you wish. Add a narrow pocket for your rod. Again, use fusible web if you don't have a sewing machine.

A series of soft pleats is easy to pinch into a strip of flowered fabric. You can buy pleater tape at the fabric section of one of those big stores that have "mart" at the end of their name. Usually the instructions are on the package. For an added touch sew a bright-colored button at each pinched point. Use pronged pleater hooks to attach the valance to the rod.

For a swagged valance, sew fringe to the bottom edge of your fabric strip. Narrowly hem the top edge and each side. Use pieces of ribbon or fabric to secure valance to rod. Arrange your panels across the rod, then catch it up with ribbon or fabric strips between the two panels and at each end. End wrapping at back and secure with pins.

To dress up windows for spring, try using grapevine wreaths. Use them as tiebacks, placing your curtain panels inside them. Add flowers or any other decorations that will complement your decor.

Arrange identical wineglasses, super-cheap at thrift stores, in a row and place a single autumn leaf, or a single flower, in each of them. Make sure your spacing of leaf or flower is as identical as possible. This is a great arrangement on a table in the dining room or on the mantel. Multiply to catch the eye!

we'd rather throw it!

It isn't the size of the space you have but how you use it that counts. Even the smallest of homes can, with a little planning and elbow grease, be made into a functional and tasteful haven. Here are some basics.

Visualize your room totally empty. This will allow you to see how to best approach a decorating plan. Look at the light that comes into the room from the windows. Are there any interesting architectural features, such as woodwork, staircase, high ceiling, etc.? Now you can decide what you want to play up and what you want to play down.

Color comes first. It can visually alter how large a space appears. To make a room look larger than it is, use a light color on the walls and ceiling. And don't be a fraidy cat. Aunt Sarie would advise good ol' safe off-white, but then again, whoever listens to what Aunt Sarie has to say. Be bold and try a soft peach or a very pastel lavender. White trim goes great with softer and lighter colors.

If you are lucky enough to have a big space, then lucky you. Paint those walls dark chocolate brown, hunter green, or deep, deep red. With darker colors, ivories and soft tans look great on the ceiling and the trim. Use high-gloss paint, it adds shine and is great to wash off.

A brief word on paint: If you have to cut cost, do it on something else, not on the quality of paint. Buy the best you can afford. The better paints are thick, go on smoother, and are more durable, and the big plus is that they almost always cover with one coat.

We all respond to specific colors differently. Ask yourself what kind of light the room you're working on has. If the sun beams in from the south, use soft, neutral colors. In north-facing rooms, let cheerful warm colors in. Sunshine yellow, bright green, etc.

When you are through painting a room, put a small amount of paint in a glass bottle, such as a baby food jar, and next time you have to do a touch-up, dip a cotton swab in paint and dab away!

Writing down what you buy

Several odd cups and saucers, ceramic pitchers, or different vases can make an eye-catching arrangement when displayed with equal spacing; turn all the handles of the cups or pitchers the same way. Repetition creates a sense of harmony in decorating.

A backsplash is an easy and inexpensive solution to splashes and splatters in the kitchen or bathroom sink area. Cut $1/8''$ hardboard to fit the backsplash space, paint with latex flat paint for the background, stencil a design on the painted board, finish it with several coats of clear high-gloss acrylic spray.

Yesterday is gone; tomorrow is a gamble; today is a sure thing— make the most of it!

If you admire hand-painted wallpaper, which is frightfully expensive, then here's an alternative. Purchase liner wallpaper, which is inexpensive, and decorate it yourself. You can stencil on it, spatter-paint or sponge-paint it. Go to your local library and check out books on other how-to painting methods.

will shock you to the sky!

To add an extra touch to a built-in bookcase, add a "border" of wallpaper or fabric around the outsides of the shelves, and back the built-in shelves with a corresponding wall covering.

Lack of storage in your kitchen driving you crazy? Look up. You probably have room to hang a rack, which could be anything from a decorative brass rod to a piece of lattice-work. Hang pots, pans, and other kitchen gadgets.

Using nonglare glass, frame a pretty piece of lace, such as a collar from your grandmother's old dress or your baby's dress. Use it as a romantic dresser tray or hang it on the wall in your bedroom.

Use a folding hat rack, the kind with 3″ or 4″ pegs, and hang pretty guest towels from the pegs.

Use a folding wine rack–they are very inexpensive–to store bathroom towels. Roll the towels up and put in the spaces where normally wine bottles would go.

Need new kitchen chair pads? Use small rag rugs, look at the local $ store, fold the rugs in half, seam them on all sides but one, turn them and insert foam pads, stitch the opening, and add chair ties.

Leftover prepasted wallpaper can spruce up your lampshades. Cut the border off the paper, moisten the strips, and apply the narrow borders to the top of the shade and the wider borders to the bottom. At no extra cost, your lampshades now coordinate with your newly papered room.

Beware of small expenses;

The bathroom mirrors in older homes often need resilvering. This can be expensive! Here's a tightwad way: If the silvering is peeling at the bottom of your mirror, turn it bottom side up. Cut designs from leftover wallpaper and paste them where the silver was peeling. If the leftover wallpaper is left from papering that bathroom, you now have a coordinated look!

A shelf behind the sofa can create a striking display space, a great place to show off favorite crafts or collectibles. Cut the shelf the same length as the sofa, from 12"- to 15"-wide lumber. For a built-in look, paint the shelf with a high-gloss enamel to match the wall color and install it an inch or two below the back of the sofa. Use the heavy-duty L-shaped brackets for support.

For a homey touch, add a shelf over the window to display plants and decorative objects.

Multiply the sunlight in a drab room with a wall of paneled mirrors. Use full-length closet mirrors, they are cheaper. Line them up side by side. Paint the frames the same color as the wall for a built-in look, or use a contrasting color for an accent.

Stencil white flowers or country silhouettes onto pastel-colored throw pillows. The effect is especially nice over small-print fabrics.

Is there one room where you spend a lot of time? Paint it. This can freshen your house in the way spring cleaning does, only more. It only takes a half a day if you don't paint the woodwork.

Buy a few bright towels for the bathroom to blend with colors you're already using. For example, add soft yellow to peach, spring green to tan, or a multicolored floral pattern to blue and white. This simple touch can do wonders for one of those "down under" days.

Use free wallpaper sample books that you can obtain from wallpaper stores for the inside of a hope chest or toy chest or box.

A doily framed in a colorful background makes a beautiful wall decor or special gift for someone.

Wrap an old pillow with new fabric and gather the ends with tied ribbons.

A stepladder or a large ladder, painted, can be unique plant stands indoors or outdoors.

Old stainless steel teaspoons screwed or glued to a drawer or cabinet make interesting handles.

Personal Wardrobe Organization

If you hate to iron something with pleats, use bobby pins or clothespins at the bottom of each pleat to hold it flat while you iron.

To reduce fading and pilling, turn clothing wrong side out before washing and drying to reduce friction on the right side of the garment.

Avoid extra ironing by hanging or folding items immediately after the dryer stops, while they are still warm.

Keep corduroy looking new by washing and ironing inside out to avoid crushing the pile.

Lose your zipper pull? That's probably that funny noise you have been hearing somewhere in your washer. Replace the pull with a colored, plastic-coated paper clip. No one will notice.

Here's a simple solution to keep buttons on children's clothes longer: Sew a small button underneath the fabric opposite a larger button. The smaller button will anchor the larger one.

When you let down a hem, it usually leaves an unwanted line on the fabric. Eliminate it by gently rubbing with a cloth dampened in white vinegar, using light brushing strokes. (Test spot first.) Then iron the hemline mark with a steam iron and a clean pressing cloth.

a mansion is built one brick at a time.

Chances are that somewhere in your house you have a where-you-put-it-until-you-can-deal-with-it-later place. Otherwise known as a disaster area. Steel your nerves, grit your teeth and grab your trash bags, we are going to clean!

With any big chore you'll need a plan of attack:

1. Break down one huge job into several mini-tasks. Divide the room into parts—floor, bookcase, chest of drawers, closet—and tackle these areas one by one, or . . .

2. Break down the job by type of chore: sorting through paper, organizing books, craft or sewing supplies.

3. Set goals you can meet. Don't expect to clear months of clutter in a couple of hours. For example: "I want to be able to see this floor by the time the kids get home from school." If you are a list maker, make a master list of individual tasks: clean off bookshelves, clear table, and so on. Check it off the list. Each check mark lets you feel you've accomplished something, and it really does give you instant gratification and will keep you moving ahead to completion.

4. Gather your gear. You don't need any fancy cleaning items, so make no more excuses about how you can't start today because your haven't got this or that.

Basic items you will need are three large boxes or shopping bags, each one labeled: give away (items you will pass on to other family members or friends); relocate (items that have strayed from their proper place, such as tools, scissors, etc.); file (papers that need to be kept, such as warranties, bills, receipts, insurance papers, and other documents that should be kept filed all together).

If you are really serious about this chore, keep a pad and pencil nearby to make notes (fix hem in blue skirt, put buttons on ed blouse, ask friend Mary if she wants baby clothes).

Choose a starting point. Pick up the easiest, most obvious trash first and get rid of it. I mean out of the room! Work through the clutter, sorting items between your boxes and trash bags. Now you can see the floor. Clean it!

To us the hardest part of the job is deciding what to keep and what to give away or throw away. We are such tightwads! Be brave and ask yourself honestly: "Do I need this?" "I paid good money for it!" "Aunt Sarie gave me this." "This will come back into fashion." "All it needs is a little . . ." "Could be worth a lot one day." Get real: If you haven't used it in forever, then get rid of it!

Feet hurt? Heels like sandpaper? Add 4 tablespoons baking soda to a quart of warm water. Soak your tootsies for 10 minutes.

Cut off the bad leg of a pair of panty hose. Do the same with another pair. Put one pair on, then put the other pair on. You now have a good pair of hose.

A half-slip pulled up under your arms makes great makeup dressing attire.

Revamp your old jewelry with nail polish.

Use a marker if you are out of eyebrow pencils.

Use Vaseline for lip gloss and makeup remover. Put a little Vaseline in a small container to carry in your purse. No need to tote the large Vaseline jars.

then we won't last!

One of us has become a grandmother! In honor of that holy state, here are a few grandmotherly tips. My sister just groaned and fainted. She thinks she is too young to be a grandmother! Ha!

When diapering baby, put oil or ointment on with one finger only and wipe the residue off on the diaper before you pin or tape.

Commercial baby powder contains simple inexpensive ingredients, like cornstarch. That's on your grocery shelf and it is cheap.

Keep masking tape near the changing table, in case those sticky tabs on disposable diapers break.

To economize, use cloth diapers for at-home days and save disposables for going out.

If you do use cloth diapers, stick the pins in a bar of soap, out of baby's reach. The soap makes the pins glide through the diaper more easily.

Remember that masking tape we told you to put on the shelf above the changing area? Stick it on their fingers or wrist. You can whip a diaper on by the time baby figures out how to get that sticky stuff off.

Here's a great distraction tool: Talk to the baby rapidly, and be dead serious. Tell him anything that's on your mind. Tell him about the weather. Before baby knows it, the dirty deed is done.

Tie toys to the high chair so you don't have to get your exercise picking up thrown objects.

Baby can practice eating messy foods or drinking from a cup in the bathtub. No water in tub, please!

Forget putting food on a plate for baby in the beginning, unless you like having flying saucers hit you in the head. Just put the food on the high-chair tray.

Put a hook on the back of the high chair to hold your cleanup cloth.

Occasionally take the high chair outside and give it a good wash-off with the hose.

Plastic ice trays are great for storing earrings, etc.

Use blush for pink eye shadow.

A mesh laundry bag is great for shampoos, soaps, toothpaste, toothbrush, etc., and can all be carried into the bathroom while at camp or traveling. You can even hang it with you in the shower.

If you need a coat, buy a classic trench coat that has a removable lining so you can get more wear out of the coat during the changing seasons. This will also give you a basic raincoat in any season.

Borrow from your man's closet; his bigger shirts and sweaters and vest will work great and add to your outfits with your suits and pants and skirts. Also you might find a few ties for that popular tie look.

If you are pregnant, sweats with drawstring pants are comfortable and perfect even after the baby is born.

Use a cigarette lighter or match to soften your too-hard pencil eyeliner. It goes on much smoother.

Baking soda is a good toothpaste substitute.

Use dental floss or fishing line to sew buttons on children's clothing. They are stronger.

generates an income of its own.

Put fingernail polish on toes and heels of hosiery if you are bad about getting runs in these areas. This is preventative.

Save on electricity and ironing. If you forget to remove clothes from the dryer, wet a washcloth and throw it in the dryer for ten minutes for wrinkles to be gone.

You can buy underwear and slips at thrift stores. Wash well.

The large decorative boxes with tops can be found at dollar stores for $1. These are great for large gift giving or for pretty storage. Barbie dolls and clothes and those miniature Barbie accessories fit nicely in these boxes and can easily be taken with the child.

Do not buy garments that need to be dry-cleaned if you cannot afford to dry-clean the garment!

Old drawers with handles make great under-the-bed storage boxes.

Keep a box that says "share" or "sell" or "store." Use the "sell" for yard sales. You can have up to three yard sales a year before you need to report your yard sale income to the IRS.

Keep your yard sale simple. Use signs that say how much clothing is, etc. Place your signs on busy streets and cover with clear contact paper for strength, weather protection, and to reuse the next time.

It's not how much you make,

Keep a basket in your car filled with stationery, pencils, paper, envelopes, stamps and address book, and utilize time spent waiting for lights, stuck in traffic jams, etc.

Use different colors of nail polish to identify your car and door keys. "D" for door, "C" for car, etc. You might want to put your initials on them also.

Your newly purchased makeup is too dark on you? Mix it with the makeup you thought was too light. You just might get the right shade.

In a hurry? Use your hair dryer to blow-dry your freshly washed panty hose. But, don't hold the dryer too close or you will be going bare-legged.

Still in a hurry? Add a dry towel to the wet items you're placing in the dryer. The wet ones will dry faster.

The top rack of a used or old electric dishwasher makes a large and wonderful spool rack for all sizes of thread. To use the rack, hang it on the wall or on a closet door near your sewing machine.

To make it easier to find those items you use most in the bathroom, glue small magnets to the walls of the medicine cabinet to hold nail files, cuticle scissors, tweezers, and other small metal tools.

it's how much you keep!

More Time-
and-Money Savers
(We Couldn't Fit
Anywhere Else!)

Each week before you leave for the supermarket, make out a check for an amount that's slightly over what you expect to spend. Put any difference between the final food bill and the amount of the check into a savings account at the bank. Thanks to coupons, two-for-one sales, and other special offers, we saved over $500 in a seven-month period!

Nothing is more hateful than a drawer that sticks. Lubricate the runners of the drawer with a candle or a bar of soap. There! One more of life's little stresses removed.

In the wintertime, keep a shoe rack by the back door. When the kiddies come in from snowball fights with soggy mittens, socks, and boots, put them on the rack to dry until the next big siege in the white stuff.

Got a knot in your chain necklace? Lay necklace on a flat surface and work at the knot with a straight pin in each hand. If you have messed it up and the knot is really a mess, use a little cooking oil on the knot and try again with the straight pins. Next time, don't throw the necklace in the drawer!

If we have to sew it,

A magic slate in the car is great for kids—no mess!!

A child's magic slate by the phone or on the refrigerator saves paper when you need to leave a note for a family member or instructions to the kids.

A burning candle will take smoke out of the room.

Use a basket for that remote control and TV guide that are always getting lost.

Kerosene lamps make great lights, decorative items, and also an important backup for when the power goes off.

A pull-out dog leash makes a great tie leash that lets your dog roam the yard. Pull the leash out as far as you need the dog to roam and click the handle to lock it. Attach the other end to a hook anchored to the house or porch or around the porch railing. Make sure it's hooked tight!

Love those long baths? Place special postcards on the back of your bathroom door, shut the door, turn on some music, and take a mini Bahamas trip.

Tape the movie channels that your hard-earned money is paying for each month! Be efficient when labeling your tapes and you will soon have a tremendous movie collection.

we'd rather throw it!

An edging around your jigsaw puzzle board keeps your pieces from getting lost as you are working on the puzzle or when you are putting it away temporarily.

Save your old car battery. It can bring at least $5.

Pour Coke over a battery that is corroded at the connection. Wipe off.

If your hair is turning gray and you keep dying it every two months, purchase a $10 frost kit and go for it! It will give you an astounding look and no one can tell where the gray is. Be sure to read your directions well. If your pull-through wand breaks, use a small regular crochet hook for this emergency.

Keep turning over your lava rocks on your gas grill. You will get more mileage out of them.

Place an advertisement for your computer skills. College kids need help and you can probably whip up that college paper in no time and make some money too. You can also help senior citizens learn computer skills in their own homes.

Sign a paper at your car insurance office stating that no one under 21 will be driving your car. You might get a savings.

A cool treat: Plastic ice trays filled with Kool-Aid and a Popsicle stick; freeze and eat!

Writing down what you buy

If your child has a B average in school, you are entitled to a car insurance discount. This applies also if your child has had any driving education.

Sell those old used hubcaps. Buy your hubcaps at a used-car-parts place. You will not believe how cheap they are, and a little sprucing up is easy to do with a Brillo pad or paint with silver spray paint.

Shoes can be resoled for a few dollars. Shoe shops repair luggage, too.

Do not buy an infant feeder for baby; cut a cross in the nipple of a regular bottle and you can use it for strained food.

Reuse window envelopes that come in your mail.

Send Christmas postcards for 20 cents instead of a card that carries the full price of a stamp.

To save on paper towels, use a new clean chalkboard eraser to wipe the insides of your car windows. Also the outsides.

Use black electrician tape or shoe polish to freshen you car trim.

Do not call a locksmith to unfreeze your car lock—heat the key with a cigarette lighter or match. Turn gently. De-ice spray you use on your windows also will work well.

will shock you to the sky!

Instead of fertilizer, help your plants with a shot of castor oil and water.

Instead of using a store-bought sharpener, sharpen your scissors by cutting through fine sandpaper a few times.

You can spend a fortune and a lifetime fighting pests. Here are a few tips we've learned:

Use hairspray on flies, bees, and insects in the house. It stiffens their wings for easier swatting.

Take a lump of sugar and wet it with several drops of spirits of camphor bought at a pharmacy when outdoors for mosquito problems.

Instead of expensive ant products, use cucumber peel on a shelf or in a drawer to ward off ants.

To keep cats out of your garden, sprinkle orange peeling.

Instead of sprays on cockroaches and ants, wash or spray cabinets with equal parts of vinegar and water.

Put peppermint around all entrances to your house. Bay leaves can be used around the pantry to keep pests away.

Soap suds can be used as an insecticide in a spray bottle.

You can extend the life of your sewing machine needle by stitching through a piece of sandpaper.

Use the 2-liter soft drink plastic bottles for convenient freezing of water in case of natural disasters or water problems.

Beware of small expenses;

Giving old and outgrown adult and children clothes to a consignment shop will bring in needed monthly income.

Does your dog need a good deodorant? Mix 2 capfuls of bath oil and 32 ounces of water in a spray bottle and rub into your pet's fur between baths.

Instead of air fresheners, place a fabric softener sheet in the bottom of a garbage pail. Also place one under the cushions of your furniture.

To deodorize a room cheaply, put a scented softener sheet in your vacuum bag.

Trade in your old paperbacks for cash or credit toward other books at used-book stores.

Putting a garlic clove in the plant pots repels plant pests.

To use your food more wisely, keep one shelf in the refrigerator just for leftovers.

Always forgive your enemies, it aggravates them.

a small leak can sink a big ship!

Never shop when you are hungry.

Instead of expensive air freshener, mix cheap liquid potpourri with water in a spray bottle. Spray on curtains, carpets, etc.

Reuse softener sheets by using spray potpourri on them.

Diaper-pin the bottoms of bedspreads and sheets instead of using expensive garters.

Notice when the garbage day pickups are for your neighborhood. Scan for furniture, crates, organizers, and things out in the open.

Use clear contact paper over special newspaper clippings you want to save, to keep them from turning yellow with age. These make excellent bookmarks when hole-punched on the corner with a ribbon or piece of yard tied on. Great keepsake or special remembrance for future generations.

A priceless tool you can buy at discount stores is a stamp you can use to mix and match letters to create a message. Purchase an inexpensive stamp pad.

Buy your sheets and blankets at the thrift store or $ store.

To make flashlights last longer, place aluminum foil between the spring and the end cap.

Place pine needles in discreet places in the house, such as the bathroom, to rid a house of fleas.

Every little bit helps;

Bathroom odors? Burn end of twine and blow out, then put in a hidden place behind the commode.

Rub the coat of your dog with olive oil every ten days or so for dry skin.

Buy two adhesive hooks for the sides of your trash can and use the free plastic bags from the store, with the handles draped over the hooks. Saves on buying smaller garbage bags.

Check your junk mail for envelopes to reuse, and for magazine pictures and coupons.

Use a standard grocery list that follows the layout of the aisles in your favorite store to save money and time.

Foods displayed at the end of the aisle appear to be on sale, but a lot of times they are not.

Try to go to the market just one day per week, and resist going back for added purchases.

You can get as many wire hangers as you need in consignment shops. Most consignment shops freely give them away.

Wash full loads rather than small loads. It saves on your water bill and also is less wear and tear on your washer and dryer.

a mansion is built one brick at a time.

Use an outside clothesline when possible. Drip-dried clothes hung on the hanger to dry are ready to put in the closet from the clothesline.

Fix the drips in your house. A leaky hot-water faucet can waste up to 800 gallons of hot water a year.

Take a shower instead of a bath for water savings.

If you just need to wash your hair, use the sink and not a whole shower.

If you have a choice, use fluorescent lights. They provide three times the light of regular bulbs.

When buying lampshades, choose thinner lampshades instead of the thicker ones for more light, thus less electricity.

Arrange your room so that one light will work for the entire room—even when you use lower-watt bulbs.

Do not block your vents with furniture.

Close your drapes and blinds to keep the sun's heat out and the heat in for the colder months. You may also just open them very little or tilted at a slant if you are the kind of person that just has to see outside.

Check your heat/air filters at least once a month during hot weather. Vacuum or replace if needed.

If we can't do it fast,

Weather-strip your doors and windows.

Fans are a great way to stay cooler with an air conditioner that can be set for summer savings. Oscillating fans are not only attractive, but provide cool air and a nice soothing sound.

Use baking soda and water and a toothbrush for corroded battery cables.

If you cannot afford scented candles, lightly coat regular candles with a spray potpourri or a cologne spray.

If you have a burn in your carpet from your cigarette, cut out the burned part and replace with a piece of carpet cut from the back of a closet.

When you buy the long package of French bread, open the package and cut the bread in half and freeze both halves together in the bag. This is good for two meals, depending on the size of your family, and you do not have to thaw out the other half or cut the bread while it is frozen.

A little perfume or cologne sprayed or dotted on a light bulb will take the place of air fresheners when you are in a pinch. Be sure the light is cool when applying this.

When a whole package of envelopes or stamps become glued together, put them in the freezer for a few hours. A knife will then quickly pull them apart.

then we won't last!

Fingernail polish on top of each little screwhead on your glasses will help keep the screws from coming out too quickly.

Aspirin tablets, pennies, or ice cubes in water will lengthen the life of freshly cut flowers.

To fool a burglar, cut out the middle of an old book and put some of your treasures inside. Place the book among your other books.

Sand in a stand-up ashtray for inside or outside use is safer from fire and is cleaner and more convenient for the smoker.

An attention-getter at a yard sale is a large box out front that says FREE FREE FREE. This gets them out of the car.

Always keep a box ready for a yard sale with your signs, change, markers, labels, etc. Sheets make great yard sale "makeshift tables" on the ground. Wrap up in the sheet any items you don't sell and save them for the next sale!

Had the misfortune to have a fire? An aluminum pie pan filled with ammonia works miracles on the smell. Try opening a bag of charcoal also to help rid the house of the fire smell.

Did you know that 15 minutes on a treadmill is equal to a 45-minute walk outdoors? The older-type treadmills are great. A treadmill does not have to be fancy to work. Older treadmills have a handle in the front center of the equipment. Purchase the inexpensive huge exercise rubber bands and tie to the handle for your upper body workout.

Write letters on solid paper and fold into thirds, then add a sticker or two to the outside of your "envelope" for the address. No envelopes necessary!

Make your own liquid soap and save gobs of money! Collect small pieces of soap and place in a glass jar. Cover the soap with water and let stand three to four days, checking to make sure the water covers the soap at all times. When the soap is soft, and a thick liquid, pour into an empty liquid soap container.

The long, 2-pocket potholders make great holders for the TV Guide *and remote when draped over the arm of a chair or couch.*

If you write a product manufacturer and ask for some coupons, they will send you some!

If you never seem to have scissors handy when you sit at the kitchen table to clip coupons, here is a good idea. Hang a basket, one with a flat side so it will fit against wall, and put scissors, ruler, pens, in it. Tie a bow on the handle to dress it up.

generates an income of its own.

Decorate a recipe file to hold receipts for items that you do buy. If the date isn't on the slip, write it there. Write the description, color and any other helpful information. If something should go wrong with the item, it is easier to return.

Instead of storing the corsages and bouquets our teenage daughters receive, hang the flowers up to dry, including the corsages with ribbons intact. After drying, arrange the flowers on a straw wreath and attach with hot glue gun or florist wire. The ribbons and lace on the corsages only add to the wreath. Hang it in her space.

There are ways to save money while saving money. Here are some of our favorites.

Deposit every check for birthday gifts into your savings.

Save each day's change. Save your pennies or change in a decorative bottle and keep in family room so everyone can contribute.

Sign up for more withholding tax than you need. It will all come back to you when you file your tax return.

Save by installments. Don't stop when you reach your goal of paying off credit cards. Keep writing those checks and deposit them in your savings account.

Join your employer's payroll savings plan. What you don't see you won't miss.

Automate your savings and investments. Arrange for a set amount to go automatically into a mutual fund or savings account each month.

Get a part-time job and save the earnings. Consider renting a room to a student.

Thinking of buying a second car? Remember you can take a lot of taxis for the price of owning, gassing, and insuring a second car—and you will still have money left over to save.

It's not how much you make,

saving energy saves more than money.
Here's what we do for our world:

Close draperies at night to keep out the cold. Open them during the day to let the sunshine in.

Vacuum or replace filters often.

Use cold water for the garbage disposal. It solidifies the grease and flushes it away more easily.

120 degrees may be adequate for your hot water. Set the dial on your pilot when you go away on vacation.

Unplug your coffeepot, iron, electric skillet, and curling iron when you're done using them.

Fluorescent lights provide 3 times the light of incandescent bulbs for the same amount of electricity. They are very economical for bathrooms and kitchens, last 10 times as long, and produce less heat.

Dimmer switches can multiply bulb life up to 12 times while reducing electricity usage.

Turn lights off when you're leaving a room.

Setting the air-conditioning thermostat at 78 degrees saves 25 percent of your home's costs.

Move furniture away from vents and window units.

Vacuum the condenser coil of your refrigerator (below or at the back of it) three or four times a year. Clean coils keep it running efficiently and help save electricity.

Limit the use of soap and the length of washing and drying cycles. Clothes only need a 10- to 15-minute wash cycle.

The best water saver for the bathroom is a low-flow toilet that uses only 1.5 to 1.6 gallons. Eventually it pays for itself by reducing water bills.

The biggest consumer of hot water in your home is the shower. Older shower heads deliver up to 8 gallons per minute. Shop for a shower head that puts out 3 gallons or less per minute.

Don't leave the water running while you brush your teeth, shave, or wash your face. Fill the sink rather than use a constant stream. This simple procedure can save your family as much as 2,000 gallons a year.

Front-load washers use 33 percent less water than top-load washers.

Don't wash a medium load on a higher water-level setting—a mistake manufacturers say people frequently make.

A faucet aerator can cut water use in half and save up to 100 gallons a year per faucet. Aerators for kitchen and bath faucets can be found in most hardware stores. They cost between $3 and $10, and simply screw onto your faucet nozzle.

On your next trip away from home, check for leaks in your water system. Write down the numbers on your water meter when you leave, and check the meter again upon returning. If it has moved at all, you have a leak.

Water your lawn and garden early in the morning. Watering during the day loses water to evaporation.

If we have to sew it,

there's no more satisfying time to save than the monthly bill-paying session. Some time- and money-savers to consider:

Order your checks directly from Checks In The Mail, Inc. (telephone 800-733-4443) and save up to 50 percent of the cost.

Order "top-stub" instead of regular checkbooks. It may cost a couple of dollars more, but you'll be able to balance your checkbook easier.

Pay off your entire credit card bill every month, when possible.

Scrutinize your credit card bills. Mistakes can and do happen.

Pay off higher-interest-rate loans first.

Make loan payments automatically from your checking account.

Obtain six to eight weeks of free credit by buying just after the billing date and paying in full just before the due date.

S H O E S T R I N G

R ecipes and Food Savers

YOU KNOW YOU'RE A TIGHTWAD...

...IF YOUR DISHWASHER WILL ALWAYS BE THE BRAND WITH TWO LEGS.

*Man cannot live on bread alone.
He needs peanut butter, too.* Us

if you don't have a Crock-Pot, then get
yourself down to the thrift store or one of the stores
that has "mart" as part of their name. (You may finish
reading our book first!) If you're a person who works,
we don't know how you have made it this far without
a Crock-Pot! The following recipes will let you have
supper ready when you arrive home from work!

Several years ago when our grandmother passed on, our mama inherited her recipes. They were in an old beat-up notebook. The pages
were yellow with time, spattered with love and spotted with tears.
Mama was soon to discover that it wasn't just Grandmother's recipes,
but more of a journal. The first "entry" was the first week she had married our grandfather! What a treasure! Written in the margins were
notes on everything from gardening to Mama and Aunt Sarie's first
steps. Our mama cried for a week after reading that book. Daddy said

he had a good mind to hide the darn thing! He didn't, and Mama kept on reading.

Some years later, when our own dear mama passed, we were given that old book of our grandmother's, and on the worn pages our mama had written her own history. She had intentionally used a different-colored ink from Grandmother's, and when we first sat down and read those notes in the margin, it was easy to distinguish the blue from the black. It is an continuing saga of the women in our family. We use green ink.

You jist cain't beat a woman that looks city and cooks country!
Irene (Granny) Ryan

One of the margin notes in Grandmother's notebook was an apparent interpretation of some of her mother's notes. This is what it said: "Mother says that a 'heap o'' something is approximately two cups, that 'two middlin' amounts o' buttermilk' is one cup, a 'smidgen o' salt' is what you can hold between two fingers, a 'pinch' of something is about three 'smidgens,' 'a right smart o'' is three 'middlin's,' and it takes five 'right smarts o'' to make a 'whole heap o'.'"

Isn't it a shame we no longer have the time to measure like that!

If we have to sew it,

Here are a few things you should be aware of when cooking with the Crock-Pot.

Some soup recipes call for 2 to 3 quarts water. Add other soup ingredients to your Crock-Pot; then add water only to cover. If thinner soup is desired, add more liquid at serving time.

If milk-based recipes have no other liquid for initial cooking, add 1 to 2 cups water. Then stir in milk as called for, and heat before serving.

You need to add milk, cream, or sour cream to the Crock-Pot an hour before the cooking is done. These dairy items tend to break down during extended cooking.

You can substitute condensed canned soups for milk, etc.; they will hold up for the extended cooking time.

A trick for thickening gravies is to take out about ½ cup liquid from the Crock-Pot, stir in the flour or cornstarch, return to Crock-Pot, and simmer on High for about 15 minutes. Or to really save time, stir in ¼ cup quick-cookin' tapioca at the start of your cooking time. The gravy will thicken as it cooks.

For stews and ragouts, usually 1 cup liquid in the Crock-Pot is enough.

If your recipe calls for cooked noodles, macaroni, etc., cook them before you add them to the Crock-Pot. Don't overcook them, just until slightly tender. That's called "al dente"! Bet you didn't know that. We didn't either!

If you're going to use beans in your recipe for the Crock-Pot, instead of soaking them overnight, cook them overnight in the Crock-Pot on Low with water and 1 tsp. soda.

Fats from meat will not drain off in the Crock-Pot. So if you are using fatty pieces of meat, they should be browned and drained before you put them in the Crock-Pot.

If your recipe calls for leaf or whole herbs and spices, it's best to use only half of what the recipe calls for. The herbs and spices have a tendency to increase in flavor. If you're using ground-up herbs or spices, add during the last hour of cooking.

Okay. Enough on Crock-Pots!
Just remember . . .
if you don't have one, get one!

here are a few tips in the kitchen we've picked up along the way.

If your homemade cookies burn on the bottom, try this: Turn your cookie sheet upside down, place dough on the bottom of the sheet. Please don't ask why, we have no earthly idea!

If you add 2 or 3 tbsp. white vinegar to your dish detergent it will be easier on your hands—and it sure makes your dishes shiny.

Don't discard those empty snack-size pudding cups. They make big ice cubes to cool that pitcher of lemonade or for the punch bowl on a hot summer day.

Writing down what you buy

Coat your pot with cooking spray before you make that homemade oatmeal or Cream of Wheat. Sure makes for a faster cleanup.

For a different taste for chocolate brownies, substitute $1/2$ tsp. of peppermint extract for the vanilla extract. Delicious chocolate-mint flavor.

He who does not mind his belly will hardly mind anything else.
Samuel Johnson

Whether you are making boxed brownies or from scratch, add a tablespoon of corn syrup to the batter for an extra fudgey taste. Bake as usual.

Use the ends or "heels" of your loaves of bread for croutons. Butter each slice, season it with some garlic salt, toast it, then cut in cubes. Use your croutons on salads or soups.

If your chocolate chip cookies flatten out when you bake them, cream the butter and sugar with a mixer, but stir in dry ingredients by hand until well mixed; then add chips. Again, don't ask use why this works. It just does!

will shock you to the sky!

Use peach preserves, apricot preserves, or red currant jelly to brush a glaze on your baked pork or chicken.

To make gravy brown, stir in 1 tsp. brewed coffee. It doesn't affect the taste, just the color.

If you're like us, when our children were school-age we were convinced that nobody but us seemed to know how to bake a cupcake. Every time we turned around it seemed like this child or that child needed a dozen cupcakes for whatever party. We got so sick of making them that one day we went into a cupcake-baking frenzy. We froze them after baking. Then on the day we wanted them, we frosted them while still frozen, sent them off to school, and they were thawed in plenty of time for the little ones to eat.

To make a fluffier omelet, add a pinch of cornstarch to the beaten eggs.

If you don't have time to make banana nut bread from those overripened bananas, then just mash them up and spread them on rice cakes. If you put peanut butter on that rice cake first, the kids will love it.

Put coffee filters in the bottom of your microwave dish before you cook bacon. They are more absorbent than paper towels.

Don't throw away those butter or margarine paper wrappers. Put them in a plastic bag in your refrigerator. Next time you need to grease a pan, grab one!

Beware of small expenses;

As a special treat, especially for holiday breakfasts, use cookie cutters to shape sliced bread for French toast. For even more seasonal flair, try adding some green or red food coloring to the egg mixture.

This is a sneaky way to get some healthful veggies and fruit into your kiddos without their knowing it! Make food look fun!

Leftovers!

What to do with leftover spaghetti?

Cut skinless, boneless chicken breasts in strips. Cook in skillet until browned. Remove the chicken and add to the skillet a package of frozen oriental stir-fry vegetables with sauce, and cook according to directions on package. Stir in the leftover cooked spaghetti and the chicken.

How about leftover rice?

Mix leftover rice with ricotta cheese. Stir in chopped pimientos, frozen green peas, and some grated Parmesan cheese. Heat in microwave or cover it and bake 325 degrees in oven until hot. All you need to add is a green salad and maybe some crusty rolls.

Leftover mashed potatoes and the end of that big ham?

Cook onions, about a $^{1}/_{2}$ cup, chopped, in butter until soft. Add the ham, chopped, and the mashed potatoes. Add enough canned chicken broth to make a thick soup. Simmer about 10 minutes. Pass the cornbread!

a small leak can sink a big ship!

Leftover veggies?

Make an omelet! Just add some cheddar or Swiss cheese and diced tomatoes. Serve it up with frozen packaged french fries.

Leftover noodles?

Toss the leftover noodles with shredded chicken and veggies with bottled Thai peanut sauce. Yummy!

Leftover turkey?

Mix 2 cups of cubed cooked turkey with an 11-oz. can of mandarin oranges and half a slice of red onion and 2 ribs of chopped celery. Pour on $1/3$ cup bottled red-wine vinegar salad dressing and toss. You can top it with chopped ripe olives. Serve it on lettuce leaves.

To make "squiggles" on top of any dessert, place melted chocolate in a zipper-lock plastic bag; cut tip off one corner of bag with scissors. Squeeze designs on wax paper, using even strokes; refrigerate. Let shapes harden, peel designs off the wax paper, and decorate to your heart's content.

If you don't feed your children lunch, they are more likely to eat what you make for dinner.

Every little bit helps;

Did you know if you cut up a few cloves of garlic and stick them in a small glass jar filled with olive oil and refrigerate them they'll last 3 to 4 weeks! Time saver!

All you tightwads, here are some fast fixes using save-the-day *ketchup!*

For an easy appetizer, brush baked chicken wings 15 minutes before they are done with ½ cup ketchup, 1 tbsp. brown sugar, apricot jam, a little vinegar, and a little soy sauce.

For a real flavor booster for broiled or grilled meats: Mash a stick of butter with 1 tbsp. ketchup; stir in 1 tsp. tarragon, shape into a log, and refrigerate until log is cold. Slice off pats from the log and put a pat on each sizzling piece of meat!

To give ketchup extra oomph, mix mustard, mayo, and pickle relish. Equal amounts of each.

For a meat loaf topping, mix ½ cup ketchup with 3 tbsp. brown sugar. Spread on top of meat loaf and make as usual.

For the best oven-barbecued chicken (actually, this is something our mama use to make) mix 1 cup ketchup, 1 cup water, 1 onion chopped, 2 tbsp. lemon juice, 1 tbsp. Worcestershire sauce, and ¼ cup brown sugar. Cook over low heat just until heated, pour over a cut-up chicken or chicken parts (like thighs, legs, or wings). Bake in a 400-degree oven for 1 hour and 10 minutes. Baste chicken while baking 3 or 4 times. Yummy!

a mansion is built one brick at a time.

and remember . . .

If there are two cupcakes left on the plate and the man takes the one with not as much frosting, he loves you. Although it could mean he doesn't like frosting!

Out of icing? Sprinkle powdered sugar through a doily, then lift off or place a solid shape on cake and sprinkle again. Remove the shape for a unique design.

Pickle cucumber slices in the leftover pickle juice and leave a few days for a different taste.

A great breadstick sauce is tomato paste or sauce (depending on how thick you would like it) and your seasonings mixed together.

Arrange your canned goods shelf in order of meats, vegetables, soups, sauces, etc., in order to glance quickly and save money when making your grocery list. Also for convenience.

Purchase a used Crock-Pot at the Salvation Army and use two when cooking: a roast and potatoes in one and vegetables in the other. Great for when you have company and you have hot wieners in one and a nacho sauce in the other.

Popcorn seasoning on regular popcorn adds the cheese flavor and is cheaper than buying the cheese popcorn.

If we can't do it fast,

Saving for a rainy day requires a longer stretch of clear weather than it used to.

Put your grill on the porch in the winter and use it. Better cooking for you and quick and inexpensive.

Tired of always peeling potatoes for the week's meals? Peel the amount of potatoes you think you will need for a week and place in a large bowl of salt water (be sure potatoes are covered with the water). Put in the refrigerator and use them throughout the week.

Carrots and celery keep longer if you place them in a large jar and cover them with water. Your family can just grab them for snacks. Change water once a week.

A 5-lb. roll of hamburger can be cut into thirds and frozen for use during the week for three meals.

Store brown sugar in the freezer and it will not harden.

then we won't last!

Cut up stale or regular bread and toast for croutons for salad or casseroles or for meat loaf filler. You can also sprinkle on seasonings before you toast for extra flavor. These may be frozen for later use.

Use a drop of vegetable oil in boiling water before adding spaghetti or noodles, so they don't stick together.

Boil equal parts of brown sugar, water, and white sugar with 2 tbsp. butter for pancake syrup.

Store your cereals, sugar, flour, cornmeal, etc., in the refrigerator if you have a problem with ants or other pests.

Buy the cheaper breakfast cereal (cornflakes, etc.) and keep raisins nearby to add to it.

Keep the few drops of fruit juice leftover in a bottle for use in basting meat. Can be frozen.

To help your crackers stay crisp, store them in a container with a dry paper towel inside.

Save leftover meat and vegetables and store in plastic Baggies in the freezer for stews and soups.

Remember that the lower-priced items in supermarkets are below eye level. Look down when shopping!

Buy nonfat generic milk to use in your cooking.

Rice is cheap and can be cooked and frozen. Run hot water over the rice to revive heat. Keep a huge bowl in refrigerator or freezer and use in a Crock-Pot with your vegetables or as a topping. No cooking when you get home!

Save margarine wrappers and use them to grease your pans and cookie sheets instead of the more expensive cooking spray.

Buy imitation bacon bits to use on your food.

Save your leftover bacon from breakfast, crush, and freeze for anything that you might want to use bacon bits on.

Instead of buying a cookie sheet, use the underside bottom of a regular baking pan.

You can get whole meals at the deli for a reasonable cost and by adding what you have at home.

Always save and freeze your leftover stews, soups, and chili to be added for other meals of the same.

Buy your bread at the day-old store. It is just one day old. Freeze and use when needed. If you do not like this bread for sandwiches, freeze it and use it for your breadcrumbs, croutons, or for meat loaf filler.

Electric skillets use half the electricity!

generates an income of its own.

Try using a thread when cutting a hot or even cool cake to avoid having the cake stick to your knife. Cuts like a charm.

Potato chips, nuts, muffins, tortillas, and breads all freeze well.

Save the few crumbs in the bottom of cracker boxes for topping on casseroles and on vegetables.

Tired of throwing away ruined lettuce? Prepare lettuce to be used for sandwiches as usual, then completely cover with water and refrigerate. Lettuce keeps longer. Change water once a week.

An elegant finishing touch for a plain white cake is to drizzle melted chocolate over white icing.

An attractive way to serve fresh fruit is to carve out a whole watermelon in the shape of a basket. Fill with fresh fruit including melon balls, seedless grapes, pineapple chunks, kiwifruit slices, halved strawberries.

Ever unwrap your cupcake and more frosting sticks to the plastic wrap than to the cupcake? Make a cupcake sandwich! Before wrapping, cut the cupcake through the center and put the top half, upside down, onto the bottom half so the frosting is in the middle. Yummy!

Push a clean drinking straw to the bottom of a bottle of sluggish ketchup. (No, don't drink it!) Pull out the straw and the ketchup will pour easily.

It's not how much you make,

If you buy "natural" peanut butter, add one or two tablespoons of honey the first time you stir it up. This keeps the oil from coming to the top, and it tastes good too!

Never throw away a newspaper before clipping coupons. Always check your ads for stores that have double coupon days. Some stores have triple coupon days every day. This is a tremendous savings. *Do not underestimate the savings of a coupon. All coupons add up to big savings.* Here are how most triple and double coupons work: 50 cents is usually worth just the face value of 50 cents. A double coupon usually goes from 34 cents to 50 cents, which means that any coupon from 34 cents to 50 cents is double off of the price. A triple coupon, any coupon *up* to 34 cents, is triple savings off of the price. Example: 30 cents off is equal to 90 cents off the price; 35 cents is 70 cents (double) off the price.

Keep your coupons current—go through them about once a week.

Take your UPC labels off of your products the minute you have finished with that product, and file them in the proper category. Keep a razor blade or a pair of scissors handy to take the UPC off. (This is the scanner code, referred to as the "UPC symbol code.") Keep your cash register receipts in your wallet, and when you store your groceries, file your cash register receipt immediately for future rebates. Rebate tickets can be picked up in most stores on their main bulletin boards. You can also find them in magazines and newspapers.

Buy your groceries at scratch-and-dent places, watching canned goods carefully but also looking for items with only crushed boxes.

You can save a lot of money this way.

When melting blocks of chocolate, grate the blocks with a cheese grater. This way, you can melt a pound or two of chocolate over a double boiler in just a few minutes. This eliminates the problem of the melted chocolate getting hard before the remainder of the block melts.

A snack that's nutritious and fun is frozen grapes. Remove the stems, wash, then lay them on a cookie sheet and freeze, uncovered. After they are frozen, put them in a bag or container, and eat away.

Corny, but—use a clean metal shoehorn to scrape kernels off an ear of corn. It's the perfect shape for the job.

Here's a simple solution to prevent cakes from cracking while they cool. Add one envelope of unflavored gelatin to the dry ingredients of any cake batter. This will prevent cracking and will also make the cake fuller. The gelatin does not change the flavor or moistness of the cake.

Apples, stuffed peppers, and tomatoes will hold their shapes if you bake them in a muffin pan. Also great for baking potatoes.

Give a pot of hot tea a different twist by adding an orange peel to the teapot a few minutes before serving.

The next time you make pancakes, add a flavored extract to the batter. Try vanilla, strawberry, almond, coconut, banana, or orange extract.

If we have to sew it,

Add ¹/₄ tsp. to batter for six pancakes or ¹/₂ tsp. for twelve pancakes.

Before you microwave bacon, place a paper plate on top. It will absorb splatters and the bacon will cook faster and more evenly.

To revive wilted lettuce, dip in hot water, then rinse in ice water with a little salt added. Shake lettuce and then refrigerate for an hour. For soggy crackers or cereal, place on a cookie sheet and bake in a 350-degree oven for a few minutes to refresh.

Add a few grains of rice to the salt shaker to absorb moisture. No more gross clumps.

Before you butter and salt your next batch of popcorn, take out a cupful and save it in a plastic bag until morning. At breakfast pour the plain popcorn in a bowl and add some milk and sugar. Puffed-corn breakfast cereal! Have you priced boxed cereal lately? Get real!

No one can worship God or love his neighbor on an empty stomach.
Woodrow Wilson

we'd rather throw it!

main meats and vegetables

spareribs 'n kraut

3 to 4 lbs. lean pork spareribs cut in serving pieces
Salt and pepper to taste
1 small can sauerkraut
1 large onion
1 apple, quartered, cored and sliced
1 tsp. caraway seeds or dill weed
1 cup water

Sprinkle ribs with salt and pepper. Brown ribs for 30 minutes in heavy skillet or broiler pan in the oven. Put alternate layers of spareribs, sauerkraut, onion, and apple in Crock-Pot. Add caraway seeds or dill weed to water and pour over all. Cover and set to Low for 6 to 8 hours (High: 4 to 6 hours. Stir several times during cooking when using the High setting only).

chicken lickin' good pork chops

6 to 8 lean pork chops, 1 inch thick
$^1/_2$ cup flour
1 tbsp. salt
1$^1/_2$ tsp. dry mustard
$^1/_2$ tsp. garlic powder (optional)
2 tbsp. oil
1 can chicken and rice soup

Dredge pork chops in mixture of flour, salt, dry mustard, and garlic powder. Brown in oil in large skillet. Place browned pork chops in Crock-Pot. Add the can of soup. Cover and cook on Low for 6 to 8 hours (High: 3$^1/_2$ hours).

super swiss steak

2 lbs. round steak, cut $^3/_4$ inch thick
Salt and pepper to taste
1 large onion, thinly sliced
One 1-lb. can of tomatoes

Cut round steak into serving pieces; season with salt and pepper and place in Crock-Pot with sliced onion. Pour tomatoes over all. Cover and set to Low for 8 to 10 hours.

For Creamy Swiss Steak: Follow recipe for Super Swiss Steak, substituting 1 can mushroom soup (10 oz.) for tomatoes. Spread soup evenly over top.

will shock you to the sky!

corned beef and cabbage
(this classic Irish favorite can be done in *one* step!)

3 carrots, cut in 3-inch pieces
3 to 4 lbs. corned beef brisket
2 to 3 medium onions, quartered
1 to 2 cups water

Put all ingredients in Crock-Pot in order listed. Cover and set to Low for 10 to 12 hours (High: 5 to 6 hours). Add cabbage wedges to liquid, pushing it down to moisten, after 6 hours on Low (or 3 hours on High).

southern-style black-eyed peas

1-lb. package dried black-eyed peas, soaked overnight in water
4 cups water
2 ham hocks or 1 smoked turkey wing
$1/4$ tsp. pepper
1 large onion, chopped
2 tsp. salt
2 stalks of celery, chopped (optional)

Soak beans in water to cover overnight. Drain and place in Crock-Pot. Add water and remaining ingredients. Cover and cook on High 1 to 2 hours, then turn to Low for 8 to 9 hours. Serve over fluffy hot rice. Please pass the corn bread!

Note: 3 packages of frozen black-eyed peas may be substituted for dried peas. Use only 2 cups of water.

here   are some more quickies!

ranchy smashed potatoes

Add a 1-oz. packet of ranch dressing mix to 4 cups prepared, unsalted mashed potatoes. Stir well and, if desired, add butter or margarine.

ranchy shake 'n bake chicken

Combine a 1-oz. packet of ranch dressing mix with ¼ cup plain bread crumbs in a plastic bag. Add 6 to 8 pieces of chicken. Shake, rattle, and roll that chicken until it's coated. Bake 50 minutes on a ungreased baking sheet at 375 degrees. Serves 4 to 6.

beefroni

Brown 1 lb. ground beef, add ½ cup mayo, a 30-oz. jar of spaghetti sauce, and a 7-oz. bag of cooked macaroni. Heat on medium, stirring occasionally. Top with cheese. Serves 4 to 6.

Add a leafy salad and some crusty bread and bingo! Supper is ready!

a small leak can sink a big ship!

We may live without friends; we may live without books; but civilized man cannot live without cooks.

Owen Meredith

chicken 'n the pot pie

2 cans of cream of broccoli soup
1 cup milk
$1/4$ tsp. thyme
$1/4$ tsp. pepper
One 10-oz can refrigerated flaky biscuits
4 cups cut-up veggies (broccoli, cauliflower, and carrots or even potatoes)
2 cups cubed chicken or turkey

In a 3-quart oblong baking dish, combine soup, milk, thyme, and pepper. Stir in veggies and chicken. Bake at 400 degrees for 15 minutes or until mixture begins to bubble. Pop that can of biscuits and cut each biscuit into quarters. Take the dish out of oven, stir it, and arrange the biscuit pieces over the hot chicken mixture. Bake 15 minutes or until the biscuits are brown. 5 servings.

Every little bit helps;

Here's a great idea, especially if the gang is in for watching the football game.

hot potato bar

Scrub and pierce potatoes with a fork. Bake at 400 degrees for about 45 minutes (if really large potatoes are used, better bake for about an hour and 10 minutes). Or arrange 1 inch apart on a microwave-safe dish or use a paper towel. Count on 8 minutes for normal-size potatoes, longer for more or bigger potatoes. To open, cut an X just through the skin on top, then push ends toward center to open. Now, the toppings.

For Ruben Topping: Corned beef, Russian dressing, sauerkraut, and Swiss cheese strips. Broil to melt cheese.

For Chill-Out Chili Topping: Heat canned chili, shredded cheddar cheese, top with sliced green onions.

For "Beachy" Topping: Drained, canned salmon or tuna, snipped fresh dill, and heated frozen creamed spinach.

For Oriental Topping: Spoon on heated canned chicken chow mein and sprinkle with peanuts.

For New York Deli Topping: Whipped cream cheese, sliced smoked salmon, and a little bit of chopped red onion.

For "Healthy" Topping: Shredded zucchini and carrots mixed with yogurt, chopped green onions.

a mansion is built one brick at a time.

crock-pot cabbage

Cover your shredded cabbage with water near the top of the Crock-Pot and season as you normally would (with a ham hock, ham pieces, or bacon grease) and cook on Low all day.

creamy scalloped potatoes

Combine in your greased Crock-Pot the following in layers, each consisting of thinly sliced potatoes (2 lbs.) then a layer of onion slices, salt, and pepper. When finished with as many layers as you want, add 2 tbsp. butter and undiluted can of cream of mushroom soup. Cover and cook on Low 7–9 hours or on High 3–4 hours. Add 4 slices of American cheese before serving. (You may substitute any cheese product you have on hand, such as shredded cheese, etc.)

beans beans and more beans!!!

Use this recipe for any kind of dry beans you would like to cook. Fill your Crock-Pot with ¾ cup water, add beans, add a huge spoon of leftover bacon grease, a ham bone, pork chop bones, ham pieces, or anything that will give flavor to the beans. Cook on Low 10–12 hours or on High for 5 hours. Make some corn bread and you have a meal! Remember, this is why it is always important to think twice before throwing away scraps such as bones, meat, etc.

baked potatoes

Fill Crock-Pot with desired number of washed potatoes and cover each potato with foil. Add about 1 cup water. Cook on Low for about 4 hours and serve a potato bar with sour cream, cheese, onions, bacon bits, chili, etc., for your evening meal with a salad.

For a cheap dinner, put a layer of tortilla chips on a cookie sheet and sprinkle with a layer of cheddar cheese and some cheap chili. Broil until cheese is melted.

meat-and-potato pie

2 prepared pie crusts (9 in.); 1 pound ground beef; 1/2 cup milk; 1/2 envelope (1/4 cup) dry onion soup mix; dash pepper; dash allspice; a 12-oz. package loose-pack frozen hash-brown potatoes, thawed. Combine meat, milk, soup mix, pepper, and allspice; mix gently. Lightly pat into one pie crust. Top with potatoes. Add top crust; seal and flute edge. Cut design in top pastry. Bake at 350 degrees about 1 hour, or till browned. Makes 6–8 servings.

shepherd's pie

1 cup frozen or canned cut green beans
1 cup frozen or canned green peas and pearl onions,
   thawed but not drained
1 carrot, peeled and thinly sliced
1 can chicken/beef broth
$1/4$ tsp. salt
2 tsp. cornstarch
2 tbsp. cold water
3 cups coarsely chopped leftover roast beef, pot roast, or steak
4 cups leftover mashed potatoes
$1/4$ tsp. paprika

Preheat the oven to 400 degrees. Mix the beans, peas and onions, carrot, and salt in a 10-inch skillet over moderate heat, and bring to a boil. Adjust the heat so that the mixture bubbles gently, cover, and simmer for 7 minutes or until the vegetables are tender. Blend the cornstarch and water in a small cup and stir into the skillet mixture. Raise the heat to moderate, and cook, stirring constantly, until slightly thickened— about 3 minutes. Stir in the beef and remove from the heat. Transfer all to an ungreased 10-inch pie pan or quiche dish. "Frost" with the potatoes and sprinkle with the paprika. Slide the pie onto a baking sheet and bake, uncovered, for 15 minutes or until bubbling and lightly browned. Serves 4.

soups, stews, and casseroles

the anybody can make beef stew

3 carrots, cut up
3 potatoes, cut up
2 lbs. stew meat, cut into cubes
1 cup water or canned beef stock
1 tsp. Worcestershire sauce
1 clove garlic (optional)
1 bay leaf
Salt to taste
$^1/_2$ tsp. pepper
1 tsp. paprika (optional)
2 onions, quartered
1 stalk celery, cut up

Put all ingredients in Crock-Pot in order listed. Stir just enough to mix spices. Cover and set to Low 10–12 hours (High: 5–6 hours).

P.S. Any time you see "optional" in a recipe, it means it is up to you whether you put it in. Leaving it out will not affect the end results.

The only reason for making honey is so as I can eat it. Winnie-the-Pooh

generates an income of its own.

chill-out chili

1/2 lb. dry pinto or kidney beans (see note at end of recipe)
2 lbs. coarsely ground chuck (brown before adding to Crock-Pot)
Two 1-lb. cans tomatoes
2 medium onions, chopped
1 green pepper, chopped
2 cloves garlic, crushed
2 to 3 tbsp. chili powder
1 tsp. pepper
1 tsp. cumin
Salt to taste

Parboil dry beans until soft; drain well. Put all ingredients in Crock-Pot in order listed. Stir once. Cover and cook on Low 10–12 hours (High: 5–6 hours).

Note: Cooking times for dried beans will vary according to their type and water hardness. For Chill-Out Chili with beans, you need to simmer the dry beans in about three times their volume of unsalted water for 30 minutes in a saucepan. Allow beans to stand, covered, for 1 1/2 hours or until softened; drain and add remaining ingredients. For all other types of recipes, cook presoaked beans in the Crock-Pot on High for 3 hours, then turn to Low.

Time cutter: Use canned beans (two 1-lb. cans), drain the liquid, and rinse the beans before adding to Crock-Pot.

Life is like an onion: You peel it off one layer at a time, and sometimes you weep.

Carl Sandburg

tater soup

6 taters, peeled and cut into bite-size pieces
2 large onions, chopped
1 carrot, cut in slices
1 stalk celery, chopped
4 chicken bouillon cubes
1 tbsp. parsley flakes
5 cups of water
1 tbsp. salt
Pepper
$1/3$ cup butter
One 13-oz. can evaporated milk

Put all ingredients except evaporated milk in Crock-Pot. Cover and cook on Low 10–12 hours (High: 3 to 4 hours). Stir in evaporated milk during the last hour. Pass the corn muffins, please!

Note: To make split pea soup, follow our recipe for Best Bean Soup, substituting a 1-lb. bag of dry green split peas for the navy beans. Soak split peas in water before cooking.

it's how much you keep!

best bean soup

1 lb. dry navy beans (soak overnight)
2 qts. water
1 lb. meaty ham bones *or*
1 smoked turkey leg or wing
Salt to taste
$1/2$ tsp. pepper
$1/2$ cup chopped celery
1 medium onion, chopped
1 bay leaf (optional)

Put all ingredients in Crock-Pot. Cover and cook on Low 10–12 hours (High: 5–6 hours).

crusty chicken cheese bake

8 skinless, boneless chicken breast halves
8 thin tomato slices
2 tbsp. melted margarine
Hot cooked rice
4 slices Swiss or American cheese
1 can cream of chicken soup
$1/2$ cup herb-seasoned stuffing

Place chicken in a 3-quart oblong baking dish. Put cheese on top of chicken. Stir soup and spread on top of cheese; top with tomato. Mix the margarine and stuffing and sprinkle on top of the tomato slices. Bake at 400 degrees for 25 minutes or until chicken is no longer pink. Serve over rice. 8 servings. For a variation on this recipe, omit the tomatoes and combine the soup with ½ cup milk.

If we have to sew it,

broccoli and rice casserole

In your Crock-Pot, combine a small diced onion (optional); 1/4 cup melted butter; 2 cups quick-cooking rice; 2 cups water; a 10 3/4-oz. can cream of mushroom soup; 1/2 tsp. salt; one 5-oz. jar sharp cheese spread (use the cheap brand); one 10-oz. package of frozen chopped broccoli.

Stir thoroughly and cover and cook on Low 7–10 hours (High: 2–3 hours). Just before serving, sprinkle cornflake crumbs browned in butter for your topping.

hodgepodge
(great for leftover vegetables that you should have saved!)

In your Crock-Pot, combine 1 lb. ground beef (you may stretch this by using ground turkey); 1 diced onion; 1 chopped pepper; 1 can tomatoes (or you can use your garden tomatoes and cook them down); 1 tbsp. sugar; 1/2 tsp. pepper; pinch of salt; one 8-oz. can lima beans; one 8-oz. can peas (or you can use any of your leftover frozen vegetables); and 1/4 cup milk.

Stir and spread one 3-oz. package cream cheese over the top of the mixture. Cover Crock-Pot and refrigerate overnight. In the morning, cook on Low 8–10 hours (High: 3–4 hours). Great idea for the night before. Dinner is ready!

There are only two kinds of foods: If it's not chocolate, it's a vegetable. —*Us*

green bean casserole

Combine in a greased Crock-Pot three 10-oz. packages frozen cut green beans (or you may substitute canned green beans); two 10½-oz. cans cheddar cheese soup; ½ cup water; ¼ cup chopped onion; ¼ tsp. pepper; 1 tsp. salt. Cover and cook on Low 8–10 hours (High: 3–4 hours). Add on the top for the last hour: cracker crumbs, cornflakes crumbs, or mashed croutons or bread crumbs.

For cheap and quick casseroles, use these ingredients: 1 can cream of chicken or mushroom soup; 1 to 2 cups leftover chicken or other meat; 2 cups cooked rice; 1 package or can of mixed vegetables or leftover vegetables. Freeze for later or warm in microwave. Add buttered bread crumbs for topping if desired.

Another cheap and easy but healthy casserole: cream of mushroom soup with 1/4 cup milk and 1 can tuna or any other can of meat or leftover meat with 1 cup shredded American cheese, 1 cup rice or noodles, onion powder. Mix and top with 1 1/2 cups of crispy rice cereal melted with butter. Can be frozen for use later.

Children love Tater Tots casserole: Mix together 1 bag Tater Tots; 1 bag frozen vegetables; 2 cans cream of mushroom soup; 2 tbsp. water, 1/2 stick butter. Put cheese on top and bake potatoes at 400 degrees for 1 hour or until done.

macaroni supper casserole

4 cups cooked macaroni (8-oz. pkg.); 1/2 cup mayonnaise; 1/4 cup diced green pepper; 1/4 cup chopped pimiento; 1 small onion, chopped; 1/2 tsp. salt; 10 1/2-oz. can cream of mushroom soup blended with 1/2 cup milk and 1 cup grated cheese (1/4 lb.). Heat oven to 400 degrees. Combine all ingredients, using only half the cheese. Pour into greased 1 1/2-quart casserole. Sprinkle with remaining cheese. Bake 20 minutes. 6 servings.

tuna-roni casserole

Use 6 1/2-oz. can tuna in place of mayonnaise in Macaroni Supper Casserole.

breads

Did you know you could make bread in your Crock-Pot? Here is one of our favorites.

brown bread

$^1/_2$ cup sifted flour
$^1/_2$ tsp. baking powder
$^1/_2$ tsp. soda
$^1/_2$ tsp. salt
$^1/_2$ cup yellow cornmeal
$^1/_2$ cup whole wheat flour
1 cup chopped nuts
6 tbsp. dark molasses
1 cup buttermilk
$^1/_2$ to 1 cup raisins

Sift flour with baking powder, soda, and salt. Stir in cornmeal and whole wheat flour. Add remaining ingredients, beat well. Pour batter into a greased and floured 2-lb. coffee can. Pour 2 cups water into the Crock-Pot, set the can inside. Place aluminum foil over the top and fold down around the edges of the can. Cover Crock-Pot and bake on High 4–5 hours. Remove and let cool 1 hour before unmolding. Slice and serve with wedges of cream cheese.

Note: This makes a great gift from the kitchen!

Beware of small expenses;

Never eat more than you can lift.
Miss Piggy

please more pumpkin bread

$^1/_2$ cup oil
$^1/_2$ cup sugar
$^1/_2$ cup brown sugar
2 beaten eggs
1 cup canned pumpkin
1 $^1/_2$ cups sifted flour
$^1/_2$ tsp. salt
1 tsp. cinnamon
$^1/_2$ tsp. nutmeg or 1 tsp. pumpkin pie spice
1 tsp. soda
1 cup chopped walnuts
$^1/_2$ cup of chopped dates or raisins

Blend oil and two sugars. Stir in beaten eggs and pumpkin. Sift dry ingredients together and add. Stir in nuts, dates, or raisins. Pour batter into greased and floured 2-lb. coffee can. Place can in Crock-Pot. Cover top of can with 6 or 8 paper towels. Place lid on Crock-Pot. Bake on High 2$^1/_2$–3$^1/_2$ hours. Don't peek until last hour of cooking!

a small leak can sink a big ship!

Note: This is another great gift from the kitchen!

Easy warm bread trick for all Crock-Pot meals: Turn your Crock-Pot lid upside down and wrap your buttered or nonbuttered bread in aluminum foil and place on top of the Crock-Pot upside-down lid. Your bread is warm and ready to eat when the Crock-Pot meal is!

any flavor biscuits

2 tbsp. instant minced onion; cheese, spices, whatever; 2 tbsp. butter or margarine, melted; 1 package refrigerated biscuits. Add your ingredients to butter; let stand few minutes. Place biscuits on ungreased baking sheet. Press a hollow in center of each biscuit with floured bottom of small glass. Fill hollows with butter mixture. Bake at 450 degrees 8–10 minutes or till done. Makes 10 biscuits.

English muffins have been popular since Day One for making individual, quick pizzas. Lightly toast the muffin first for extra crispness. Then top and toast again just to heat everything through. You can do the same thing with pita pockets split in half. One advantage of these mini-pizzas—they'll fit into a toaster oven.

Every little bit helps;

salads

pineapple and lime ring

One 3-oz. pkg. lime gelatin
1 cup boiling water
$^1/_2$ cup cold water
1 tbsp. lemon juice
$^1/_2$ cup nuts
One 8-oz. pkg. cream cheese
1$^1/_2$ cups miniature marshmallows
Two 8$^1/_2$-oz. cans crushed pineapple, drained

Dissolve gelatin in boiling water; add cold water and lemon juice. Gradually add gelatin to cream cheese, mixing well. Chill until thickened but not completely set; fold in marshmallows, pineapple, and nuts. Pour into a 6-cup ring mold or a 13×9×2-inch dish; chill until firm. Unmold if using a mold, or cut into squares if using a dish.

heavenly hash salad

1-lb., 1-oz. can pitted sweet cherries; cup of fresh seedless grapes or 8$^1/_4$-oz. can of grapes; cup small marshmallows; $^1/_2$ cup blanched almonds, walnuts, or pecans; $^1/_4$ cup mayonnaise; $^1/_4$ cup sour cream; 1 tbsp. brown sugar. Mix all ingredients together. Refrigerate.

a mansion is built one brick at a time.

kids' food specialties of all kinds

cheeseburger stuff

1 lb. ground beef
3/4 cup chopped onion
1 can condensed cheddar cheese soup
1 cup frozen mixed veggies
1/4 cup milk
2 cups Bisquick
3/4 cup water
1 cup shredded cheddar cheese (only if you want!)

Heat oven to 400 degrees. Grease a 13×9×2-inch baking dish. Cook the ground beef and onion in a skillet until beef is brown. Drain off the grease. Stir in the soup, veggies, and milk. Stir Bisquick and water in the

The great man is he who does not lose his child's-heart. Mencius

If we can't do it fast,

baking dish until moistened; spread it evenly in the dish. Spread the beef and onion mixture over the batter; sprinkle cheese on top. Bake 30 minutes. Serves 8 to 10.

here's a quickie when unexpected company drops in.

velveeta salsa dip

Microwave 1 lb. Velveeta cheese, cubed, and one 8-oz. jar of salsa in a 1½-quart microwavable bowl on High for approximately 5 minutes, or until cheese is melted. Stir after 3 minutes.

Serve hot with assorted cut-up veggies. Makes about 3 cups of sauce.

nachos by chicken

This one is so fast, you'd better have everybody at the table!

1 can of cheddar cheese soup
½ cup salsa
Two 5-oz. cans chunk chicken
Sliced, pitted ripe olives
1 bag (about 10 oz.) tortilla chips
Sliced green onions

In saucepan mix soup, salsa, and chicken. Use low heat and stir occasionally. Serve soup mix over chips. Top with green onions and olives. Serves 6. You might want to heat those chips before you add the chicken mixture.

then we won't last!

Kid Tips
fun-filled pretzels

One 11-oz. tube soft breadstick dough
Filling: peanut butter, shredded cheese, or chopped dried fruit
$1/4$ cup of melted apple jelly
Topping: poppy and sesame seeds, nuts, toasted coconut,
    chopped dried fruit

Preheat oven to 350 degrees. Grease a baking
sheet. Separate 2 strips of dough and flatten each to
$1/2$ inch width. Spread 1 tsp. of filling down the center
of 1 strip. Top with second strip. Pinch edges to seal.
Shape. These shapes can be worms, snails, funny circles, etc. Place on prepared baking sheet. Repeat with
remaining strips.

Bake for 15 minutes, until lightly browned. Place
on rack to cool. Brush with the apple jelly; decorate
with the toppings. Makes four big pretzels.

If you have trouble getting your children to get a
decent breakfast, here's one you should try. Fill an
ice-cream cone half full of yogurt. Layer bananas,
strawberries, raisins, or other fruit. Fill the rest of the
cone up with more yogurt, then sprinkle on a topping
of crushed cornflakes.

They will think they are getting something they're
not!

dirt cups with worms

2 cups cold milk
1 pkg. chocolate instant pudding
One 8-oz. tub whipped topping, thawed
One 16-oz. pkg. chocolate sandwich cookies, crushed
8 to 10 plastic 7-oz. cups

Pour milk into large bowl, add the pudding mix, beat until well blended. Let sit 5 minutes or so. Stir in the whipped topping and $\frac{1}{2}$ of the crushed cookies. Place 1 tbsp. crushed cookies into the cups. Fill the cups $\frac{3}{4}$ full with the pudding mixture. Top with remaining cookies. Refrigerate 1 hour. Decorate with Gummi worms and frogs.

Take our word for it, they look rather disgusting but the children will love them!

These make great birthday party favors or Easter favors.

The first thing I remember liking that liked me back was food.
Rhoda Morgenstern

generates an income of its own.

birds' nests

$^1/_2$ stick ($^1/_4$ cup) margarine
One 10-oz. bag regular marshmallows or 4 cups miniature marshmallows
6 cups crispy rice cereal
Nonstick cooking spray
Colored paper, toothpicks, and jelly beans

Melt margarine in pan over low heat. Add marshmallows and stir until completely melted. Remove from heat. Add cereal and stir until well coated. Spray 16 muffin cups with cooking spray. Press cereal mixture over the bottom and up the sides of the cups. Cool. Remove from cups. Write guests' names on flags made of colored paper, attach to toothpicks, and insert in cups. Fill "nests" with jelly beans.

spunky-faced pitas

One 8-oz. container pineapple cottage cheese
$^1/_4$ cup whipped cream cheese
$^1/_2$ cup mixed fruit pieces
$^1/_4$ cup walnut pieces
4 small pita pockets (white or wheat)
Shredded carrots, grapes, banana slices, apple slices

Combine cottage cheese and cream cheese in a blender. Whirl until smooth. Stir in fruit and nuts. Open pitas and spread $^1/_4$ of filling in each. Now decorate the faces of the pitas. Use a banana slice for the eyes, lay half a grape on the banana slice (that's the eyeball), add an apple wedge as a smiling mouth, sliced celery curves for the eyebrows, a grape for the nose. Stick celery sticks or carrot curls on top of the filling in the pita for the hair. Eat a pita!

funky craft dough you can eat

1 cup butter or margarine softened
6 hard-cooked egg yolks, mashed
2 tsp. cream of tartar
5 cups all-purpose flour
1 cup shortening
$2^1/2$ cups sifted powdered sugar
2 tsp. baking soda
1 tbsp. vanilla extract
Red, yellow, green paste food coloring

Cream butter and shortening; add sugar, beating until light and fluffy. Add the egg yolks, soda, cream of tartar, and vanilla, beating well. Add flour a little at a time, mixing well.

Divide the dough into 4 equal parts. Color one part red, one yellow, one green, and leave the last dough part plain. Wrap each part up separately in plastic wrap and chill at least 1 hour.

Here's the part the children love! They can hand-shape the dough into anything they want, or roll out the dough and cut it with cookie cutters. Bake their creations at 350 degrees for 8 to 10 minutes. Let the cookies cool on the baking sheet for a few minutes.

teddy bear puddin' faces

One 6-oz. box chocolate pudding and pie filling
2³/4 cups milk
³/4 cup mini-marshmallows
Single-serve graham cracker crusts (6 come in one pkg.)
12 vanilla wafers
18 mini-marshmallows
4 yellow candy jelly rings, 3 cut in half and 1 sliced thin

Prepare pudding according to the package directions, using 2³/4 cups milk. Let stand a couple of minutes. Stir in the ³/4 cup mini-marshmallows. Spoon pudding into each of the 6 crusts. Shortly before serving, add vanilla wafer ears, marshmallow noses, half jelly-ring mouths and sliced jelly-ring eyes.

Instead of giving the kids the "same ol', same ol'," in their lunch boxes, try some of these ideas!

Inside-Out Sandwich: Roll a slice of luncheon meat and a slice of cheese around a commercial breadstick. Tell the kids it's called a "Crunch-wich."

Stuffed Apple: Slice off the top of an apple. Hollow out the core, leaving the bottom of the apple intact. Fill the apple with peanut butter mixed with raisins, cream cheese, chocolate chips or nuts. Put the top back on the apple and pack in a sandwich bag. Your kid will be the envy of every other kid at the school table.

Parents believe in heredity, until their kids start acting goofy.   U⁴

piggies in their blankies

2 cups Bisquick
8 hot dogs
1/2 cup cold water

Heat the oven to 450 degrees. Mix Bisquick with cold water until a soft dough forms; beat it well for about 20 strokes. Form the dough into a ball, place on floured board, and knead a few times. Roll the dough into about a 13-inch circle. Cut circle into 8 wedges (like a pie). Place a hot dog on each wedge of dough; roll up, beginning at the wide end of the wedge. Seal by pinching the point of the dough into roll. Bake on an ungreased cookie sheet for about 15 minutes or until light brown.

more lunch box ideas!
Peanut Butter Switch: When you make the next peanut butter sandwich, exchange graham crackers for the bread. Children love this tasty and crunchy surprise.

we'd rather throw it!

Funny Fillings: Add unusual ingredients to conventional sandwich fillings.

- Add raisins, coconut, crushed pineapple, or honey to peanut butter. This is also good on crackers.
- Chopped nuts, celery, green pepper, pickle relish, olives, sunflower seeds, and onions perk up tuna, salmon, or chicken filling.
- Mashed avocado, with a few drops of lemon juice, crisp bacon pieces, and chopped onion make a great filling. Or use this as a dip and pack chips or carrot and celery sticks.
- Mix mashed banana, peanut butter, and a little frozen orange juice concentrate together for an unusual bread spread.
- Cream cheese mixed with chopped celery, nuts, and raisins creates a great sandwich. Put the filling on wheat bread.
- Any of the above fillings can be stuffed into the small sandwich pitas.

To make chocolate curls, pour melted chocolate into a foil-lined pan. Refrigerate till hard. Rake a cheese slicer across the hardened chocolate to make chocolate curls!

'Fess up: You really don't feel invigorated after aerobics. You crave a jelly doughnut and a nap.

For cheese cookies for kids, mix $1/4$ cup shredded cheese, $1/4$ cup softened margarine, 1 cup flour, $1/2$

tsp. salt. Knead dough and chill. Roll into balls and bake for about 15 minutes. Makes about 3 dozen.

snake cake

Bake a cake in a tube pan or meat loaf pan. Make three. Put them on a platter to form an S shape. Cut a 2-inch segment off the tail. Cut this segment into two triangles. Place the two triangles at one end to form a head with open jaws. Attach these pieces with a little frosting. Frost the entire cake in green, then add candy eyes, etc.

sandwich wheels

Cut the crusts off slices of pumpernickel or white bread. Then, with a rolling pin, roll the slices out lightly and spread thickly with cream cheese. Place a stick of celery across one end of each slice and roll up tightly. Wrap the rolls in foil until just before eating. Then cut them into $1/2$-inch slices to serve.

south american bananas

$1/4$ cup of confectioners' sugar; 2 tsp. cocoa; 4 bananas; $1/2$ cup chopped nuts (walnuts, pecans, or almonds); 4-oz. tub whipped topping. Sift sugar and cocoa. Peel the 4 bananas and cut them in half. You will have 8 halves. Roll each banana half in the cocoa sugar until it is well covered. Put the banana halves on a serving plate. Sprinkle nuts and coconut on top of bananas. Refrigerate and top with whipped topping. Serves 4.

cantaloupe sailboats

Large cantaloupe; 8 scoops vanilla ice cream (2 pints ice cream); 2 slices store-bought pound cake. Cut the cantaloupe lengthwise in half. Scoop out the seeds and pulp and throw them away. Cut the cantaloupe halves lengthwise again to make 4 pieces. Cut each of the 4 pieces crosswise in half. You will have the 8 pieces of cantaloupe you need. The cantaloupe pieces will look a little bit like boats. Put a piece of cantaloupe on each plate. Put a scoop of vanilla ice cream in the middle of each piece of cantaloupe. Cut the 2 slices of store-bought pound cake diagonally in half. You will have 4 pieces of cake. Cut each piece in half again, as in a triangle. You will have 8 cake triangles. Put 1 toothpick in the center of each scoop of ice cream. Put 1 cake triangle on top of each toothpick. The cake triangle is the sail, and the ice cream and melon are the boat. Eat right away, before the boats sail away. Serves 8.

Make a Teddy Bear Cake using one small cake for the head, a larger one for the body, cookies for ears, and ladyfingers for the arms and legs. Cover with butter icing, positioning candy for eyes and nose.

maple-flavored snack

⅓ cup peanut butter, ⅓ cup maple-flavored syrup, crackers. Put peanut butter into measuring cup up to ⅓ line. Into that same cup, pour maple-flavored syrup up to ⅔ line. Mix slowly but thoroughly with fork. Spread on crackers. (Spreads about 12 large crackers.)

magic potion

For a very fizzy effect, freeze chocolate chips and place a few at the bottom of each glass. Then fill the glasses with soda.

rainbow cake

Cut a round cake in two, stand up and stick together with icing. Decorate.

If you want life to run smoothly, you must grease it with peanut butter! us

sun cake

Surround a round cake with ladyfingers and wafer cookies.

caterpillar cake

You will need about 4 jelly rolls for this cake. Cut each little jelly roll into smaller ½-inch sections and stand them up on a plate. Cover a small dome-shaped sponge cake in icing for the head.

Lions and Tigers and Bears, Oh My! Add animal crackers to the rim of your next pumpkin pie or spice cake. Remember to add the little animals after you bake the pie or ice the cake, but not more than 1 hour before serving, so they won't absorb too much moisture.

Forgotten this old-time goodie? It's one the kids love! For roasted pumpkin seeds, after the kids have totally destroyed the kitchen carving their pumpkins, wash and separate seeds from the strings and pulp. Spread the seeds on a cookie sheet, sprinkle with a little cooking oil and salt. Bake for about 15 minutes in a 350-degree oven.

quick fruity cake

1 No. 2 can (2½ cups) any fruit pie filling; 1 pkg. loaf-size yellow-cake mix; ⅓ cup butter or margarine, melted. Spread pie filling in buttered 9×9×2-inch pan. Sprinkle cake mix evenly over top of filling; drizzle with butter. Bake in moderate oven (350 degrees) 40–45 minutes or till top is golden brown. Serve warm with ice cream. Makes 9 servings.

peanut butter pudding

¼ cup peanut butter; 2 cups milk; one 4¼- or 4½-oz. pkg. instant chocolate pudding. Beat peanut butter and ¼ cup milk with rotary beater (or in mixer) till smooth. Slowly add remaining milk, beating until well blended. Add pudding mix; blend well, about 1 minute. Pour into serving dishes; chill.

basic white cake

2½ cups cake flour, sifted; 2½ tsp. baking powder; ½ tsp. salt; ½ cup butter; 1¼ cups sugar; 1 cup milk; 1 tsp. vanilla; 4 egg whites, stiffly beaten. Preheat oven to 375 degrees. Butter and flour pan. Combine cake flour with baking powder and salt. In a large bowl, cream butter and sugar. In a separate bowl, combine milk and vanilla. Add this and the flour mixture to the butter mixture alternately, beating after each addition. Gently fold in egg whites. Pour batter into pan. Bake for about 25 minutes, or until a toothpick inserted into the center comes out dry.

a mansion is built one brick at a time.

apple treats

Carefully remove the core and seeds from the center of the apple. Using a spoon, stuff the apple with peanut butter. Lay the apple on its side, and cut it into 4 or 5 slices. Arrange the slices on a pretty plate.

fruit mix

Combine applesauce, pineapple, some raisins, a few walnuts, and a bit of cinnamon in a mixing bowl. Stir, gently, with a wooden spoon. Chill the mixture in the refrigerator for at least 4 hours. Serves 4–6. Enjoy this dish plain or topped with whipped cream. How about adding some vanilla ice cream? Or try it topped with yogurt and a handful of granola!

ice-cream pie

1 quart vanilla ice cream (softened until mushy); 9 whole graham crackers, coarsely broken; 14 bite-size ($1/4$ oz.) chocolate bars (plain, crunchy, or nut), coarsely broken (or 3 regular bars); $1/2$ cup coarsely chopped unblanched almonds or walnuts; 1 prepared 9-inch chocolate or graham cracker crumb crust. Spoon the ice cream into a large bowl and gently fold in the graham crackers, chocolate bars, and almonds. Spoon the mixture into the crumb crust and smooth the top. Garnish, if desired, with additional crackers, chocolate bars, and almonds. Freeze until firm— about 2 hours. Serves 8–10.

To extend the amount of punch if you are running low, add additional lemon-lime soda, ginger ale, or champagne.

basic frosting for spreading

¼ cup butter; ¼ cup milk; confectioners' sugar. Melt butter and add milk. Beat in enough confectioners' sugar to make frosting thick enough to spread easily. Makes enough to frost one 9-inch layer cake.

basic dark chocolate frosting

6 tbsp. softened butter or margarine; ¾ cup dark cocoa; 2⅔ cups confectioners' sugar; ⅓ cup milk; 1 tsp. vanilla. In a small mixing bowl, cream softened butter or margarine. Add cocoa and confectioners' sugar alternately with milk. Beat to a spreadable consistency. Add more milk as needed. Blend in vanilla. Makes about 2 cups of frosting.

basic decorator frosting

½ cup shortening; 1½ cups confectioners' sugar; 2 tbsp. milk. Cream shortening with confectioners' sugar. Stir in milk. Beat well, adding more sugar as needed to make a stiff enough consistency for use in a pastry bag. Makes enough to frost one 9-inch layer cake.

then we won't last!

drinks

quick banana drink

2 medium-ripe bananas; 2 cups milk; 2 large scoops vanilla ice cream. Break banana into blender container. Blend till smooth, about 15 seconds; scrape down sides. Add milk and ice cream. Buzz till blended, about 15 seconds. Serves 3–4.

fruity fruit all-occasion punch

Pour 2 cups orange juice and 2 cups pink lemonade into a pitcher. Add a small can of pineapple chunks and the juice in which they are packed. Add 1 cup strawberries to the pitcher, taking care first to cut any large strawberries in half. Peel a navel orange and separate it into sections. Cut each section in thirds and add them to the fruit punch. Fill the pitcher with ice cubes. Stir the punch with a wooden spoon until the pitcher is frosty. Serve this fruit punch with straws and a spoon.

fruit milk shake

1⅓ cups cold fruit juice (whatever you choose); 2⅓ cups cold half-and-half cream or milk; 1 tsp. cinnamon. Pour fruit juice into 4-cup measuring cup up to the 1⅓-cup line. Pour into quart jar. Pour cream into the same measuring cup up to the 2⅓-cup line. Add to juice. Dip the teaspoon measuring spoon into cinnamon and sprinkle it over juice and milk mixture. Fasten lid so that it stays tight. Shake jar about five times, and count as you do it. Pour into tall glasses. Serves 4.

cranberry punch

1 quart cranberry juice; one 46-oz. can pineapple juice, one 6-oz. can frozen lemonade concentrate; ¾ cup sugar; two 28-oz. bottles lemon-lime soda or ginger ale. Combine all ingredients except the soda or ginger ale in a punch bowl and chill. Just before serving, add the soda. Also add a garnish of lemon slices, a fruit-ice ring, or scoops of lemon or pineapple sherbet, if desired. Makes about 36 half-cup servings.

sparkling punch

4 6-oz. cans frozen lemonade concentrate; four 9.6-oz. cans frozen pineapple juice; 1½ quarts cold water; 2 quarts sparkling water; 3 quarts ginger ale; slices of fresh fruit. Combine the juices and water, then chill. Just before serving, add the ginger ale and sparkling water. For extra interest, add ice cubes made from fruit juice or ginger ale or put in scoops of lemon, orange, or lime sherbet. For a champagne punch, substitute champagne for the ginger ale and sparkling water. Makes about 50 half-cup servings.

generates an income of its own.

quick party punch

2 quarts lime sherbet; three 1-liter bottles lemon-lime soda or ginger ale. Just before serving, scoop softened sherbet into the punch bowl. Slowly pour the soda or ginger ale over the sherbet. For extra color, add lemon-lime soda ice cubes with maraschino cherries in each or a fresh fruit ice ring, if desired. Makes about 36 half-cup servings.

To extend the amount of punch if you are running low, add additional lemon-lime soda, ginger ale, or champagne.

milkshakes

12 oz. (350g) fresh fruit; 2 tbsp. superfine sugar, 1½ pints (900ml) milk; 4 scoops vanilla ice cream. Place half the fruit, sugar, milk, and ice cream in a blender or food processor. Blend for 20 seconds, then pour into a pitcher. Repeat with the remaining ingredients. This recipe makes 2 pints (1.2 liters) of natural, creamy milkshake. Serve in tall glasses with straws.

A delicious drink for a cold winter's night is hot lemonade, and it feels soothing to a sore throat too. Just add boiling water to a teacup and add lemon juice and honey to suit your taste.

Everybody knows what a great warmer-upper hot chocolate is. Ever heard of hot vanilla? It is yummy! Heat up a cup of milk, stir in 1 or 2 tsp. sugar and ¼ tsp. vanilla extract.

holiday specialties

for Halloween and for the kiddies . . .

ghosts in the graveyard!

3^1/$_2$ cups milk
2 pkgs. (4-serving size) chocolate-flavor instant pudding and pie filling
One 12-oz. tub whipped topping, thawed
One 16-oz. pkg. chocolate sandwich cookies, crushed. (You can take out all
  of your frustrations by putting those cookies in a zipper-lock bag and
  beating them with a rolling pin! Yeah!)

Make pudding as directed on package using 3^1/$_2$ cups of milk. Let set 5 minutes. Stir in 3 cups of the whipped topping and half of the crushed cookies. Spoon the mixture into a 13×9-inch dish. Sprinkle the rest of the crushed cookies on the top. Refrigerate at least 1 hour. To decorate the "graveyard," use some rectangular-shaped cookies for tombstones and glob some spoonfuls of whipped topping for the ghosts. Scatter around the graveyard some corn candy and candy pumpkins.

Admit it: You have fed your children cereal for dinner.

a cake for the red, white, and blue day!

2 pints strawberries
1 store-bought pound cake, cut into 8 slices
1 $1/3$ cups blueberries
One 8-oz. tub of whipped topping, thawed

Slice 1 cup of strawberries: halve the remaining ones. Set aside. Line the bottom of a 12×8-inch glass baking dish with the cake slices. Top the slices with 1 cup of the sliced strawberries, 1 cup of the blueberies, and the whipped topping. Arrange the strawberry halves and the remaining blueberries over the whipped topping to create a flag design. Line the strawberries up for the flag's red stripes and fill in the upper left corner with the blueberries for the stars. Keep your cake refrigerated until ready to serve. Serves about 15. It is great on a hot Fourth of July afternoon.

for an easy easter dessert!

$2/3$ cup boiling water
$1/2$ cup cold water
Ice cubes
1 ready-made graham cracker crust
1 pkg. (4-serving size) strawberry gelatin
One 8-oz. tub whipped topping, thawed

Stir boiling water into gelatin in large bowl until dissolved. Mix cold water and ice cubes to make 1¼ cups. Add to gelatin, stir until slightly thickened. Remove any remaining ice. Stir in whipped topping. Refrigerate 10 minutes until mixture will mound. Spoon into crust. Refrigerate for 4 hours or until firm. Decorate with a ring of whipped topping around the edge of the pie, add some pastel-colored jelly beans. If you like, sprinkle a little coconut around the edges.

for a great Thanksgiving dessert!

pumpkin pie elite

2 frozen deep-dish pie crusts
2 eggs
One 16-oz. can solid-pack pumpkin
One 12-oz. can evaporated milk
$3/4$ cup plus 2 tbsp. sugar, divided
3 tsp. pumpkin pie spice, divided
$1/4$ cup chopped walnuts

Preheat oven and baking sheet to 375 degrees.

In a large bowl, whisk together eggs, pumpkin, milk, $3/4$ cup sugar, and 2 tsp. of pumpkin pie spice. Pour this filling into one frozen crust. Bake on preheated baking sheet 30 minutes.

While it is still frozen, crumble the second crust into small pieces; toss the pieces with the remaining 2 tbsp. of sugar, and the 1 tsp. of spice and the walnuts. Sprinkle topping evenly over the pie. Bake an additional 30 to 40 minutes, or until knife inserted in center comes out clean. Serves about 8.

we'd rather throw it!

The only time you ever lose weight is after you finally give in and buy something that fits.

us

christmas red and green poke cake

1 pkg. white cake mix
2 cups boiling water
1 pkg. lime gelatin
1 pkg. strawberry gelatin
One 16-oz. can vanilla frosting

Heat oven to 350 degrees. Mix the cake, bake and cool as instructed on the cake mix box for two 9-inch-round cake layers. After they cool, place cake layers, top sides up, in two clean 9-inch-round cake pans. Poke cake with a large fork at $1/2$-inch intervals.

Stir 1 cup of the boiling water into each flavor of gelatin in separate bowls 2 minutes or until dissolved. Carefully pour red gelatin over 1 cake layer and lime gelatin over second cake layer. Refrigerate 3 hours.

Dip 1 cake pan in warm water 10 seconds; unmold

onto serving plate. Spread with about ¼ of the frosting. Unmold second cake layer; carefully place on the first layer. Frost top and sides of cake with remaining frosting.

Refrigerate 1 hour or until ready to serve. Store leftover cake in refrigerator.

here are some more goodies for Santa Claus time!

fruity creamy cheesey squares

1 cup sugar, divided
¹/₃ cup butter
1¹/₂ cups graham cracker crumbs
One 21-oz. can blueberry filling or topping
Three 8-oz. pkgs. cream cheese
4 eggs
1 tsp. vanilla extract

Heat oven to 325 degrees. To prepare crust: In saucepan place ¼ cup sugar and the butter; heat until butter is melted, stirring occasionally. Stir in graham cracker crumbs; press mixture evenly over the bottom of a 13×9-inch baking pan. In a large bowl, with an electric mixer beat cream cheese until smooth. Gradually beat in remaining ¾ cup sugar. Beat in eggs, one at a time, and vanilla, until well blended. Spoon the blueberry filling evenly over the crust. Carefully pour cream cheese mixture over blueberries. Bake just until set, about 45 to 50 minutes. Cool. Chill until cold, about 2 hours. Cut into 24 squares.

will shock you to the sky!

christmas cherry cheese pie

Mix two 8-oz. pkgs. of cream cheese, softened, $\frac{1}{2}$ cup of sugar, $\frac{1}{2}$ tsp. vanilla. Add two eggs. Pour into 1 prepared graham cracker crumb crust (6-oz. or 9-inch). Bake at 350 degrees for 40 minutes or until center is almost set. Cool; refrigerate for 3 hours. Spread with one 21-oz. can cherry pie filling. Makes 8 servings.

shimmering super punch

To make this great punch, thaw two 12-oz. cans of frozen cranberry-raspberry juice cocktail juice concentrate and chill two 1-liter bottles of orange-flavor carbonated water. Mix it just before serving. To make it shimmer, float spiced-apple rings and stars cut from orange peel on the surface.

It's holiday time, the boss is coming to dinner and you want to put on the dog! Okay. Serve the following!

For dessert: Melt squares of chocolate in the microwave (no more than 30 seconds at a time or you'll burn it). Coat the inside of a foil muffin liner with the melted chocolate. Refrigerate. After chocolate hardens, remove the liner. What do you have? A little chocolate cup! What are you going to with it? Mix up some of that instant box pudding, chocolate or vanilla, and fill the little chocolate cup. To make a special garnish for putting on top of the pudding, brush some melted chocolate on a leaf, a real leaf—preferably one that is not poison. Refrigerate. When chocolate is hard, peel the leaf off. Stick into the pudding, add a raspberry or strawberry at the leaf base. The boss will think you've slaved in the kitchen all day!

Here's our favorite. Our mouths are watering! Holding the stem end of a clean, dry strawberry, dip into melted chocolate, let excess drip off. Cool to harden on wax paper; store in refrigerator until serving time. Yeah!

Make your own decorative Christmas tree cake. For a square cake, cut it in half, making two triangles, and add M & M's for ornaments. For a rectangle cake, cut away pieces, making a tall Christmas tree. Add candy "ornaments" and raisins or chocolate chips for the trunk.

Make your own Fourth of July cake in a rectangular cake pan; cover with blueberries for the blue part, strawberries for the red, and white frosting for the white part.

Buy or bake a large batch of cookies and divide into baggies (that fold over). Tie with ribbon and add a homemade tag (from your old cards) for excellent favors or thank-yous or Christmas neighbor gifts.

a small leak can sink a big ship!

SHOESTRING

Ideas for Children's Rooms

in this section we will be giving you some ideas for children's spaces. It's important for kids to have a place that is their place, to play in and to dream in. We know from experience that it is not always possible for each child to have his or her own room, but with a little planning and creativity, a place can be found, even if it is only a corner in a room.

If you have more than one child sharing a room, a **room divider** is definitely in order. Many thrift stores and junkyards have old doors. Take a series of these, often 3 or 4 will do the trick, and hinge them together for a screen. Of course, you don't leave it freestanding, if your children are anything like ours were, that screen will be standing for approximately a minute and half! Attach hooks to the ceiling and corresponding hooks to the top of the door screen. Attach a chain between the ceiling hook and the door screen hook. Put a simple strip of wood, on the floor, on each side of the screen. Anchor it well and the bottom of the screen will remain on the floor where it is supposed to be.

Another option for a screening effect is to stretch a sheet between two rods. One rod is mounted on the ceiling, the other mounted on the floor. Depending on the height of your ceilings, a king-size flat sheet usually does the trick.

A *garden trellis* is another idea. Instead of roses growing on it, you can hang stuffed animals, masterpiece drawings from your offspring, etc. The trellis will need to be framed with two-by-fours and then attached to the ceiling and floor.

Floor-to-ceiling bookshelves work really well.
Remember, you will need the shelves placed back-to-back if you're
dividing the room down the middle. Again, you need to secure the top
to the ceiling and the bottom to the floor, and it is a good idea to fasten together the bookcases at their sides. The clerk at Wal-Mart will
be able to tell you what kind of fasteners to use.

Imagination...
is the true magic carpet.
Norman Vincent Peale

If you are encouraging your children to read, give them an inviting
place in their room to do so. One of our friends found an old claw-
footed bathtub in the junkyard! She painted it shiny bright yellow and
filled it with plump pillows covered in bright colors of the rainbow!
That kid lived in that tub! That was a number of years ago, and that little boy today is an English teacher!

Wonder what happened to that tub?

Create a wall that's okay to write on. Install a big chalkboard and supply colored chalk. Or attach a sheet of white laminate
to the wall. Use erasable markers to draw with and supply a soft cloth
to erase with.

Every little bit helps;

While you're decorating your child's space, keep in mind his or her **HEIGHT!** Hang artwork, mirrors, and wallpaper borders at kids' eye level. And low storage might encourage your child to keep a space neat. We said "might," didn't we?

A cheap and the most creative way to perk up your child's room is to paint a colorful **mural.** If you feel you can't paint freehand, then borrow an overhead projector to enlarge a picture onto the wall. Trace with pencil and fill in with acrylic paints.

Use a high-gloss paint for **easy wipe-down** of walls and woodwork.

Paint walls a medium shade that resists smudges and fingerprints.

Use a bright-colored sheet for the bedspread, or an old quilt. Our Big Sis used a crochet tablecloth, which she found at a $ store for under $10, on her little girl's bed.

Curtains, valances, and pillows to scatter across the bed can all be made from sheets or pillowcases. Coordinate the whole room with just sheets. Your best buy for linens for this purpose are the $ stores!

Instead of putting up curtains, **LAMINATE** a window shade with fabric or wallpaper.

Find ready-made furniture to nest together, or create your own space-saving units with bunk beds and a chest of drawers.

a mansion is built one brick at a time.

A great decor for a boy's room is the **locker room look.** Paint the walls a high-gloss enamel (brown, deep gold, or navy, with ivory or soft yellow woodwork). And for storage for toys, clothes, sports equipment, etc., use actual army or gym lockers. Look at surplus stores for all kinds of neat finds. Upright lockers, footlockers, even small tents. What are you going to do with a tent? You just put it up in one corner of your son's room and stand back and watch! He will be playing army, fort, and even spaceship until the cows come home. Do the cows still come home? Whatever! You know what we mean.

$\mathcal{R}$*ecycle* the bed rail or ladder from former bunk beds; hang it on the wall for displaying decorative items, or add hooks for baseball caps, etc.

Cut wallcovering and borders into mats for pictures. Use extra wallpaper borders to edge a door or window frame.

If you're lucky and your child's room is large, then take advantage of the space by putting up a bright colored **T E N T.** Make the theme of the room "Circus." A wallpaper border of either clowns or animals would add to the feel! Or…

Put up a brown tent and add a wallpaper border of jungle animals. A rattan floor mat and, yes, a few fake plants standing tall in the corners would only add to this theme. Or…

Create a "Noah's Ark" theme, whether you build an "ark" bed or just gather all those stuffed animals onto a shelf over the bed, you can achieve this look. Find a picture of Noah and his animals in a

If we can't do it fast,

coloring book, rent or borrow that overhead projector, and paint it on one wall. Make it so that the giraffe's head touches the ceiling. Big!

For a little girl's room, ruffle fabric on a mirror frame or a dressing table to match bedspread and curtains, and toss lots of frilly pillows on her bed.

Paste wallpaper borders to the front of drawers or on top of a chest. The paper is easily removable when you update the decor.

Apply a heavy vinyl wallcovering to one wall in your child's room, let this wall be for posters, etc., that older children like to push-pin into the wall. The pin holes won't show when they decide to "re-arrange" their "display."

Don't forget under the bed for out-of-sight storage for toys, seasonal clothing, etc.

Paint and trim an old *steamer trunk.* All those doors and drawers can store lots of Barbie stuff!

If "country" is your look, collect a row of **bushel baskets** for toys and stuff.

Stack games in plastic milk crates to keep them neat and tidy.

Garbage cans come in bright colors. Use one for all those hard-to-store items like baseball bats, hockey sticks, or tennis rackets. No, you cannot put the lid on. You can't have everything!

then we won't last!

On a day when your nerves are "steeled" up, let your child dip his or her hand in bright acrylic paint and hand-print a border in their room. Tell them they definitely have to **STAY IN THE LINES!** To be on the safe side, stand by with soap and water!

Hang a fishing net or hammock in the corner for toys, or for your child to dream in.

A lovely touch to add to a little girl's room is to display antique-looking clothing and old straw hats or bonnets. Hang them on a board with wooden pegs for hangers. Or...

Instead of wooden pegs, glue on large wooden spools, the kind that thread used to be on. Or...

Instead of wooden pegs or wooden spools, use old antique-looking doorknobs as hangers!

For a clever and inexpensive way to decorate with wallpaper, take a border design and frame sections of it. How about a section of border, the design being hats, hung above the display of antique-looking clothes and hats!

The Nursery

An old wicker basket makes a great *bassinet.* Paint with a bright-colored nontoxic paint and decorate with ribbons and lace. Use the basket later for toy storage, as a laundry basket, or even a wagon—add wheels and a rope for pulling!

Drawers lined with soft blankets are ideal for a tiny baby. Make sure the bottom is firm like mattress, not soft like a pillow.

A large shelf (3′ × 5′), mounted on the wall waist-high, covered with a pad, makes a great **changing table.**

Slip a pillowcase on the changing table pad. The pad will stay clean and all you have to do is change the pillowcase.

Use a pad on top of a dresser for changing baby. For a safety belt, take an old belt, cut it in half, and staple or tack the two ends to the top of the dresser.

Delicately embroidered handkerchiefs, pieced together and quilted or tied, make a lovely *coverlet* for baby. Border the coverlet in a soft pastel.

Collect some of your resident artist's drawings and trace them onto plain white pillowcases. Embroider them in the colors he or she has used in the drawings. Later it makes a nice keepsake.

generates an income of its own.

If there always seems to be a pile of **dirty duds** next to your child's changing table and you don't want a clothes basket out in view, take an old wooden nail keg and line it with printed fabric to match the rest of the nursery. Paint the keg a soft color or leave it natural.

If you don't want to climb up a ladder and stand forever on tiptoes while you stencil or paint a border around the nursery, use wallpaper lining—it's plain white—and do your thing on it. Then maybe you can talk your husband into hanging it for you. Just add paste to the back of the liner and stand aside and tell him how to do it!

If the stuffed animals are piling up, here's an idea.
From your local carpet dealer, get a big cardboard tube that carpet is wrapped around. (He will give it to you free!) Measure your child's room from floor to ceiling and cut the tube to the same measurement. Paint or cover the tube with wallpaper or adhesive-backed paper. Screw cup hooks into the cardboard in various places up and down the tube. Then stand the tube in the corner of the room. Hang the "animals" on the hooks with ribbons that are tied around their necks.

The gorgeous gift wrapping paper out today is great for running two strips from the ceiling to the floor behind a bed for a headboard.

Use a small string mop or a commode mop, and paint, to swab color on an ugly ceiling or wall.

Make a new pillow for your child's room with a favorite T-shirt. Stuff the T-shirt's stomach and chest area with a pillow. Fold back the arms and the bottom hem to the back of the pillow. Sew.

It's not how much you make,

For a cheap focal wall in a kid's room, staple or tack the **FUNNY PAPERS** onto it.

Outgrown tennis shoes make great little holders for tiny plants in a child's room with the top of a hairspray container as the inside pot.

Make a headboard by wrapping any size board with fabric and nail to wall. Great headboard for a mattress on the floor.

Use a sponge and paint to give character to a chest or wall.

Cover one focal wall of room with fabric or old sheet. Pink the edges and glue, staple, or tack to wall.

Make a desk between two old short filing cabinets and paint them a bright color. Use a door or board from thrift store as the desktop.

Make your own lower closet pole by using an old broom handle cut to length and two long shoestrings, rope, or chains. Check people's trash on trash day for used brooms, etc., for this idea.

Splatter-paint a white sheet or fabric and staple to a board to match room.

Splatter-paint a wall. *Revamp* furniture by splatter-painting.

Use bright-colored poster board as a bulletin board.

Rather than block more of the window than necessary with a valance or drapes, use sheers to hide only the **poopy view.** Add a shelf above the sheers and decorate with plants, collectibles, or, in a child's room, toys.

Loop fabric over center of rod, then carry a section over each end. We've seen this window treatment done in white mosquito netting in an all-white bedroom. Talk about *Out of Africa!*

Another idea for leftover prepasted wallpaper: Cut out simple folk-art shapes from the paper. Trace around a cookie cutter or use the characters in a child's coloring book—trace shapes or color them and mount them for a border design.

Take a cutlery tray, turn it sideways, and hang it on a wall. It makes excellent *shelving* for collections of small objects, such as thimbles or those little cars our kids like to collect.

Convert your child's old toy chest into a hope chest. You'll **BOTH** be glad you did!

SHOESTRING

Nuggets of Wisdom

YOU KNOW YOU'RE A TIGHTWAD...

...IF CASHIERS PUT UP THE "LANE CLOSED" WHEN IT'S TIME TO CHECK OUT WITH YOUR COUPONS!

in our Tale at the beginning of this book, we told you that we too have known rough times. During those times we have leaned on our faith and our family, but in addition we firmly believe that it is only you who can pick yourself up, dust yourself off, and move on, that only you can achieve the goals you set for yourself.

Find the "switch" that works for you and act on it. When we have lost our perspective and then our direction, the following nuggets of wisdom helped to right us once again. We hope that they might encourage you too.

For Every Thing There Is a Season

For every thing there is a season, and a time
to every purpose under heaven.

A time to be born, and a time to die; a time to plant,
and a time to pluck up that which is planted;

A time to kill, and a time to heal; a time to
break down, and a time to build up;

A time to weep, and a time to laugh;
a time to mourn, and a time to dance;

A time to cast away stones, and a time to
gather stones together, a time to embrace, and time
to refrain from embracing;

A time to get, and a time to lose; a time to keep,
and a time to cast away;

A time to rend, and a time to sew; a time to keep silence,
and a time to speak;

A time to love, and a time to hate; a time of war,
and a time of peace.

Ecclesiastes 3:1–8

If we have to sew it,

and remember . . .
Never lose your sense of humor.

May those who love us, love us
And those that don't love us,
May God turn their hearts;
And if He doesn't turn their hearts
May He turn their ankles
So we'll know them by their limping.
              An old Gaelic blessing

Blessed are they who can laugh at themselves,
for they shall never cease to be amused.
              Unknown

a woman's wisdom: thoughts on life and love

The more I wonder...the more I love.
              Alice Walker

Love is like a violin. The music may stop now and then, but the strings remain forever.
              June Masters Bacher

The giving of love is an education in itself.
              Eleanor Roosevelt

Joy is a net of love by which you can catch souls.
              Mother Teresa

we'd rather throw it!

The best and most beautiful things in the world cannot be seen or even touched. They must be felt with the heart.
Helen Keller

Life is the first gift, love is the second and understanding the third.
Marge Piercy

and remember . . .
to show compassion

Our mama use to quote to us this simple poem from McGuffey's Second Reader.

Beautiful faces are they that wear

The light of a pleasant spirit there;

Beautiful hands are they that do

Deeds that are noble, good and true;

Beautiful feet are they that go

Swiftly to lighten another's woe.

Writing down what you buy

and our big sis's favorite:

If I can stop one Heart from breaking

I shall not live in vain

If I can ease one Life the Aching

Or cool one Pain

Or help one fainting Robin

Unto his Nest again

I shall not live in vain.

Emily Dickinson

and for the ultimate in compassion read:

The parable of the Good Samaritan.
The Holy Bible
The book of Luke
Chap. 10, Verses 29–37

will shock you to the sky!

and remember . . .

Our most important responsibility . . .
that of our children.

"Over in the Meadow"

Over in the meadow,
In the sand, in the sun,
Lived an old mother toad
And her little toadie one.
"Wink," said the mother;
"I wink," said the one;
So she winked and she blinked
In the sand, in the sun.

Over in the meadow,
Where the stream runs blue,
Lived an old mother fish
And her little fishes two.
"Swim," said the mother;
"We swim," said the two;
So they swam and they leaped
Where the stream runs blue.

Over in the meadow,
In a hole in a tree,
Lived an old mother bluebird
And her little birdies three;
"Sing," said the mother;
"We sing," said the three;
So they sang and were glad,
In the hole in the tree.

Beware of small expenses;

Over in the meadow,
In the reeds on the shore,
Lived a mother muskrat
And her little ratties four.
"Dive," said the mother;
"We dive," said the four;
So they dived and they burrowed
In the reeds on the shore.

Olive A. Wadsworth

*Making the decision to have a child—it's momentous.
It is to decide forever to have your heart go walking around
   outside your body.*

Elizabeth Stone

a small leak can sink a big ship!

and remember . . .

To work . . .
To stick to it . . .
To have courage . . .

Work while you work,

Play while you play;

One thing each time.

That is the way.

All that you do,

Do with your might;

Things done by halves

Are not done right.

                    From the McGuffey's primer

Mr. Meant-To has a comrade,

And his name is Didn't-Do;

Have you ever chanced to meet them?

Did they ever call on you?

These two fellows live together

In the house of Never-Win,

And I'm told that it is haunted

By the ghost of Might-Have-Been.

                    "Mr. Meant-To" by
                    Benjamin Franklin

Every little bit helps;

and remember . . .

Try, try again . . .
It's never too late . . .

For of all sad words of tongue or pen,
The saddest are these: "It might have been!"
                    John Greenleaf Whittier

It is never too late to be what you might have been.
                    George Eliot

Don't be afraid of the space between your dreams and
    reality.
If you can dream it, you can make it so.
                    Belva Davis

We learn the rope of life by untying its knots.
                    Jean Toomer

Life is what happens while you are making other plans.
                    John Lennon

and remember . . .

Confidence is painting the ceiling after installing the new carpet.   *Us*

a mansion is built one brick at a time.

and remember . . .

Don't say can't . . . say can
You may have to fight a battle more than once to win it.

Margaret Thatcher

The word impossible is not in my dictionary.

Napoleon Bonaparte

The World is a great mirror. It reflects back to you
what you are.
If you are loving, If you are friendly, If you are helpful, the
World will prove loving and friendly and helpful to you.
The World is what you are.

Thomas Dreier

Real difficulties can be overcome; it's the imaginary ones that are unconquerable.

us

If we can't do it fast,

this book is an attempt to tell you how we have saved time and money. Sometimes *saving* really isn't enough, and you need to make a few more dollars. It happens to all of us.

We have a permanent garage sale. How? One side of our garage is lined with cheap shelving we picked up at the dump, thrift stores, and flea markets. We have several fold-up tables, these are sawhorses with plywood on them. All the items are categorized, cooking junk together, trinkets, furniture, toys all have their own space. Each item has a price on it. And in one box are things we know aren't going to sell and there is a sign on that box that says FREE and it is always in a prominent place on our table. Our cash for making change is always ready and in a pouch we wear around our waist. That way we are free to float around and chat with our customers without being constantly worried about who is watching the cash box! We are open only one day a week! Everyone knows about us and we no longer have to run an ad in the classifieds. A sign is on the garage and there is another one in front of the house. A cute name helps! How about "Susie's Saturday Sales," or "Annie's Attic Adventures"!

There are lots of ways to earn money. Here is a list of a few of those creative ways. Remember most of these skills are in good demand, and if you are already skilled or can develop a skill, they are a great way to increase your income.

then we won't last!

- Gardening/yard work
- Organizing and catering parties
- Preparing income tax returns
- Altering clothing
- Pet-sitting
- House-sitting
- Baby-sitting
- Dog-walking
- Painting/wallpapering
- Word processing
- Teaching exercise classes
- Tutoring
- "Gofers" for busy families
- Crafting
- Bookkeeping
- Housecleaning
- Cleaning offices
- Organizing and performing at children's parties
- Storytelling

and remember . . .

In digging others out of trouble, you can find a place to bury your own.

SHOESTRING

Games

YOU KNOW YOU'RE A TIGHTWAD...

... IF YOUR CHILDREN DO NOT OWN A BOOK WITHOUT SOMEONE ELSE'S NAME IN IT.

There was a little girl

Who had a little curl

Right in the middle of her forehead;

And when she was good

She was very, very good,

But when she was bad she was horrid.

Henry Wadsworth Longfellow

in this section we are going to talk about games. Games to make for our children, games to play with children, games and times that they will always remember. Uncle Ed use to play Kick-the-Can with us! Daddy hung us a swing from the big oak in the backyard and Mama played HopScotch with us. Aunt Sarie threw dishwater on us when we got in her flower bed and Cousin Con tied us to the clothesline post and squirted us with his water pistol, which didn't have water in it at all, but red Kool-Aid; we thought we were bleeding to death. Well, we were only five! What else would a five-year-old think!

Little Golf: Make safe golf clubs by attaching a stiff sponge to a yardstick or sawed-off broom handle; use rubber bands to attach. Dig some holes in the ground and put a container, like a yogurt or snack pudding cup, in the hole. Place barriers like outdoor toys or flower-pots between "tees," a mark on the ground, and holes. Use a real golf ball or a Whiffle-type ball.

Clue and Sleuth (a variation of good ol' hide-and-seek)**:** The seeker closes her eyes and counts. The hiders leave clues to where they are hiding: like an arrow on the ground made from twigs, or twigs spelling out the name of the hider, or a chalk drawing on the driveway or side-walk showing some significant clue to the whereabouts of the hider.

Funny Totem Pole: Cut off the tops of milk cartons, then cut 2-inch slits in the corners so the bottom of one container can be wedged inside the top of another. See how many can be stacked without falling! You might want to put a rock in the bottom of the first container to keep the "pole" from falling over. Unstack the cartons and have the children cover them with paper sacks. Then they can decorate them with colorful designs, faces, or cut-up pictures from magazines. Restack after decorating and stand back and watch them admire their totem pole!

That Crazy Ball: Tape a coin to the side of a small foam ball. Toss the ball in the air and see how crazy it acts. Try different-size coins, a penny, a nickel, a quarter; or try two coins. Try playing catch with it and see what happens.

No Bases Baseball: Players throw a rubber ball or a tennis ball at targets made out of stacked-up boxes, piled rocks, etc. Easy hits are singles, harder ones doubles, and so on. If you miss the target, you get an out. When a player has 3 outs, the next thrower comes to bat.

The Sandbox: You don't need to build an elaborate structure for a sandbox. Use a wading pool, a cardboard box lined with a plastic drop cloth; even an old dishpan can hold enough sand for a good time. Give the kids buckets, cups, plastic cars or animals, and a pail of water. Those kids will build mountains, tunnels, rivers, jungles, raceways, railways, etc.

Can we deduct our husbands as a child expense?

Us

here's what you can do if you have a "neat" cardboard box and a little imagination.

Cut a hole in the top of a large box, large enough to fit over your child's head and shoulders. Staple lightweight rope or strong ribbon to the carton to make shoulder straps. Draw and cut out a horse's head on cardboard or poster board. Cut flaps in the "horse's" neck.

it's how much you keep!

Cut a slit in the carton, push the neck into the slit, and tape the flaps down from inside the carton. Staple yarn to make the mane and tail. **Ride 'em cowboys!**

On a rainy or snowy afternoon a bunch of boxes can be a lifesaver. Save cereal boxes, oatmeal boxes, toothpaste boxes, laundry soap boxes, gelatin boxes, pudding boxes, etc. This is your child's "grocery store." Stack a few big cartons, one on top of the other, for the grocery's shelving. Put the groceries on the shelf, set up a cash register—this could be an old calculator taped on top of a cigar box filled with play paper money and real pennies! Provide some sacks for those groceries. Put prices on the boxes and get the children to add them up for the total. If you really want to be mean, let them figure out the tax!

Give the princess a handful of **elbow macaroni,** a shoelace, a tiny brush, and some poster paints. Tell her to make a necklace. P.S. It

You're only young once. After that, you have to make up some other excuse for your stupidity.

U4

If we have to sew it,

takes a long time to paint those little macaronies!

Have the kids remove the lid from an egg carton, the Styrofoam kind, and fill the little compartments with potting soil and seeds. Put the little garden in a sunny window and watch it grow!

For the **"I'm bored"** crowd, make a peanut necklace. Cut a length of strong thread about 4 inches longer than you wish your finished necklace to be. Thread a fine needle and push the needle through each peanut (use peanuts in the shell). When all the peanuts are strung, remove the needle and tie thread ends together. Let them paint them with poster paint or Magic Markers. You have covered the kitchen table with plastic, haven't you? Otherwise, polka dots may be your new look in the kitchen.

and remember . . .

Today, rather than cleaning your house or doing the laundry, do something spontaneous with your children. Go to the park, go exploring in the woods, go to Uncle Ed's barn and see the new kittens, whatever. They will remember!

here are a few "educational" games, just don't tell the kids they are educational.

For ABC's as easy as 1-2-3, use a stack of index cards, print each letter of the alphabet on one side and paste pictures of things that begin with that letter on the other. You can let your child help by searching through magazines and cutting out pictures he likes. Use the index cards like flash cards. Show the pictures and ask what the letter is, or vice versa.

Have your child estimate how many bites it will take to eat an ice-cream cone; then have her count how many bites it actually takes.

Before going to a **zoo,** ask your child to choose an animal and look up information on that animal. Learn with the child what the animal eats, where it lives, etc. It will make the trip more interesting and fun.

Take a walk in the neighborhood; ask your child to read the house numbers and tell you if they are **odd or even** numbers.

Set up a thermometer and have your child check it each day. Have her write it down.

Take your child for a walk and tape-record the sounds (tape recorders are an easy and inexpensive find at thrift stores). Play the tape for his friends, brothers, and sisters.

Encourage your child to save a portion of his weekly allowance. Count the money together each month and name the coins. We did this with one of our daughters, and when the end of the month came and we were to count the coins, there was quite a decrease in the amount that should have been there. When we asked where was the rest of the money, she replied, "That was the Lord's money, Mommy, and he told me to buy an ice-cream cone so as I wouldn't lose my senses!" We wonder where in the world she got such an idea? Did we ask you?

Writing down what you buy

A teenager is a person who answers the phone in the middle of the first ring. *Us*

for older children:

Take a script of a children's play and have your child and their friends memorize their lines and make the sets for the play. Stage the play for neighbors and friends. They pay, you serve refreshments.

Encourage your child to **write letters** to a long-distance cousin, friend, or grandparent in the summer when school is out. Tell them they have to use cursive writing for practice. They will hate you forever.

For young artists who want to draw on the wall, mount a roll of paper on brackets. Did you know you can get paper rolls from the Dumpster behind your local newspaper's office? They are called ends and they throw them away. Cut matching brackets from wood and mount securely to the wall. Slide a wooden dowel through the paper roll, and set into the brackets. **Let her roll!**

will shock you to the sky!

Mama always says, "Don't eat the paint." Guess what? This paint you can eat! Prepare instant chocolate pudding according to package directions. Place a piece of paper over newspapers or plastic and make a picture on the paper. Then lick your fingers!

Here's a play dough you can eat! In a bowl mix 2 cups of peanut butter, 2 cups powdered milk, and 3 tbsp. of honey. If too sticky, add more powdered milk, a little at a time. You can even add raisins or nuts. **Play and eat!**

Here's one you **can't** eat! In a bowl combine 2 tsp. cooking oil, 1 cup salt, and 1¹/₄ cups water. Gradually add 2 tbsp. cornstarch and 3 cups all-purpose flour. Knead until smooth. Divide the dough into parts and add a different food coloring to each part. Add small amounts of water if dough is dry, or flour if dough is sticky.

To make homemade finger paint, in a saucepan combine 1 cup of all-purpose flour and 1 cup of cold water. Stir until smooth. Add 3 cups of additional cold water. Cook and stir a minute more. Remove from heat and pour into three heat-proof bowls. Use food coloring to make those colors! Cover with plastic wrap and let stand at room temperature till cool. Spoon paint on paper; paint!

Cut 10 holes about ¹/₂ inch wide through a box top that's about 12 inches square. Insert a clothespin in each hole and number them from 1 to 10. You will need 6 rings. They can be small embroidery hoops, jar rings, or wooden curtain rings. The child kneels about 5 feet from the box and tries to toss the rings over the clothespins. The player with highest score after 10 tosses wins.

Beware of small expenses;

This would be a wonderful world if people showed as much patience with a child as they do in waiting for a fish to bite.

Us

Our kids are great at this game, but can they change a toilet paper roll? No! Too complicated!

To make a **felt storytelling board** for a preschooler, gather scraps of colorful felt or flannel material, a box that is bigger than a shoe box, say a boot box, craft glue, and scissors. Cut a piece of felt or flannel to fit inside the lid of the boot box. You might want to pick a neutral color to do this, say a soft or pastel blue. Cut the scraps of felt or flannel into figures, which will stick to the felt background of the lid. Make trees, birds, fish, flowers, stars and even letters. People and animals can be made up of several shapes, so be sure to cut circles out for eyes and noses, and rectangles for arms and legs.

You can also clip magazine pictures or coloring book characters. Glue the cutouts to cardboard, cut around the shape and on the back glue a small strip of sandpaper. They will stick to the background felt on the box lid! When your child is finished with the "board," pack the felt figures in the bottom of the box and put the lid on. This makes a great toy for the car!

The right temperature at home is maintained by warm hearts, not hot heads.

Us

for more "boredom busters" in the car . . .

Before you go, make a list of things you might see along the way: types of cars, animals, buildings, etc., and you might pick some items that are specific to your route: a pond, a restaurant, that big red barn, an outdoor market, etc. Give the list to each child, as they see the item have them check it off their list!

When our children were small, before every trip, we would make what we called a **"car box."** The kids could hardly wait to get to the highway so they could delve into their boxes. In what was actually a plastic dishpan, we would put a box of colors, a new coloring book, a pencil with paper to draw on (add a clipboard to put that paper on), several books, a tiny little toy (such as little people or cars) and a tape

Every little bit helps;

recorder with earphones. The tapes are stories that were recorded by us ahead of time. All of these items are available at your $ store! Often you can get 4 coloring books for $1!

An old small suitcase makes an excellent car carrier for **kid entertainment** items.

Flat plastic buckets (with the middle handles) placed in the trunk make for excellent organization and fewer things rolling around. This also works for organization in the car and for those mini-trips to keep the kids busy; fill with **"busy-kid things."**

Don't throw away old window shades. They make great play mats for the kids. After removing the shade from the roller and trimming any torn edges, you can draw any sort of scene with a waterproof marker. Draw a play town including a pond, streets, sidewalks, parking spaces, etc. Scale it to match your child's favorite cars or trucks. On the reverse side of the shade draw mountains, a forest with paths, a cave, and a river. A great place for those little men. When playtime is over, the shade can easily be rolled up and stored.

Save old jeans or anything with pockets to make a "busy" cloth book to hold crayons, small books, small dolls, small Bible, etc., for your child when traveling or waiting in doctors' offices, church, etc.

Do not buy watercolor paints. Mix 1 tbsp. water, 1 tbsp. dishwashing liquid, and 1 tbsp. food coloring.

a mansion is built one brick at a time.

Play dough recipe: 1 cup sifted flour, $^1/_2$ cup salt, 3 tbsp. oil, and 1 small package of Kool-Aid. Add 1 cup boiling water and stir and knead into a dough.

Build a dollhouse from stacked shoe boxes using wallpaper samples, old pieces of tile or carpet. Tape boxes together. Use catalogs for pictures.

Use 2-liter bottles as **bowling pins** for your child.

An outgrown playpen makes a great toy chest. Put the playpen down on one side for easy access.

Use laundry baskets for toy boxes in coordinating colors. **Cheap.**

Make dollhouse stools by draping a piece of material over an empty spool and place a rubber band over the fabric for a draped look.

Tie a shoestring to an empty laundry basket for a child's **make-believe wagon.**

Make your own tape of stories for your child to listen to at night or while traveling. (Also works with regular books for adults.)

Save all old squirt bottles for outside **water play.**

Make dollhouse or puppet people by saving Popsicle sticks and put real-life pictures from magazines and catalogs for faces.

If we can't do it fast,

Tie a ball onto a branch of a tree to "ball-target practice."

String boxes together with shoestring and tie to tricycle for a long train. Animals and dolls can ride.

Draw a clown on a large box and cut a hole for the mouth. Make **beanbags** by folding fabric around beans and wrapping tight with rubber band.

Make miniature puzzles from old fun memory snapshots glued on cardboard. Cut into puzzle pieces and keep in envelope with name on front. Also use magazines or poster pictures.

Use a brown paper bag for a puppet. Use the end crease for mouth. Add eyes, etc.

Make an **obstacle course** with old tires. Tires can also be painted.

Use poster board or recycled cardboard and magazine pictures to create a memory game (shapes, letters, pictures, etc.).

Glue felt to the top of a shoe box and put felt pieces and shapes inside the box for an instant felt board game.

For your child, put some pebbles in an empty salt container for a noisemaker.

Oatmeal boxes make excellent **drums.**

Popsicle sticks make great dollhouse shutters.

then we won't last!

part two

free

(and almost free)

tidbits

from the

tightwad twins

YOU KNOW YOU'RE A TIGHTWAD...

...IF YOUR CAT AND DOG EAT THE
SAME FOOD!!

lawyers

The leading directory of lawyers, Martindale-Hubbell, has put its listings on the Web *(http://www.martindale.com)*. For no charge, learn where your lawyer went to school, what jobs he's held, and his specialty practice areas.

christmas tags

Christmas tags are free every year in your December issue of most women's magazines.

car help

For a back issue of *Consumer Reports* annual auto buyer's guide, send $5.00 to Consumer Reports, P.O. Box 2015, Yonkers NY 10703. This is a must before you buy used or new!

For a printout of dealer cost on base price and options of any car, send $12.00 to *Consumer Reports* Auto Price Service, P.O. Box 8005, Novi MI 48376.

For $2.00 per minute, a national car pricing and referral service can give you instant dealer base prices on most automobiles. The live operator can answer most of your questions, too. The number is 900-226-CARS.

u.s. savings bonds: now tax-free for education

Write to the Consumer Information Center, Attention R. Woods, Pueblo CO 81009. Cost: 50 cents.

free credit help

National Foundation for Consumer Credit
8611 2nd Avenue
Suite 100
Silver Spring, MD 20910
(800) 388-2227

Family Service America
Public Inquiry Specialist
11700 West Lake Park Drive
Milwaukee, WI 53224
(800) 221-2681

Fair Credit Reporting (Free)
Federal Trade Commission
Public Reference Branch
Room 130
6th and Pennsylvania, N.W.
Washington, DC 20580
(202) 326-2222

real estate properties and investment

To find a qualified real estate appraiser, check your local Yellow Pages or contact the Appraisal Institute at (312) 335-4100.

The Basics of Interest Rates (Free)
The Federal Reserve Bank of New York
Attention: Public Information
13th Floor
33 Liberty Street
New York, NY 10045
212-720-5000

Buying Lots from Developers (Free)
Department of Housing and Urban Development (HUD)
Program Information
451 Seventh Street, S.W.
Washington, DC 20410
(202) 708-1420

insurance

Consumer's Guide to Disability Insurance (Free)
Consumer's Guide to Long Term Care Insurance (Free)
Consumer's Guide to Medicare Supplement Insurance (Free)
Health Insurance Association of America
1025 Connecticut Ave., N.W.
Washington, DC 20036
(202) 223-7780

Medigap: Medicare Supplemental Insurance
(Publication #D14042, Free)
> American Association of Retired Persons (AARP)
> Fulfillment Department
> 601 E Street, N.W.
> Washington, DC 20049
> (202) 434-2277

Guide to Health Insurance for People with Medicare
> Medicare and Prepayment Plans
> Consumer Information Center
> Attention: S. James
> Pueblo, CO 81009
> (719) 948-3334

Medigap Insurance
> Health Care Financing Administration (HFCA)
> 6325 Security Boulevard
> Baltimore, MD 21207-5187
> (410) 786-3000

> National Insurance Consumer Organization
> 121 North Payne Street
> Alexandria, VA 22314
> (703) 549-8050

aging and continuing care
Consumer's Directory of Continuing Care Retirement Communities
> American Association of Homes for the Aging
> AHA Publications
> 901 E Street, N.W.
> Suite 500
> Washington, DC 20004-2037
> (202) 783-2242

Consumer Information on Continuing Care

American Association of Retired Persons
Research Information Center
601 E Street, N.W., A2-402
Washington, DC 20049
(202) 434-6240

National Council of Senior Citizens
1331 F Street, N.W.
Washington, DC 20004
(202) 347-8800

How to Choose a Home Care Agency

National Association of Home Care
519 C Street, N.E.
Washington, DC 20002-5809
(202) 547-7424

Directory of Accredited Home Care Aide Services and All About Home Care

Foundation for Hospice and Home Care
519 C Street, N.E.
Washington, DC 20002-5809
(202) 547-6586

National Alliance of Senior Citizens (a senior citizens' lobbying group; write for information in becoming a member)

1700 18th Street, N.W.
Suite 401
Washington, DC 20009
(202) 986-0117

college financial aid

Applying for Financial Aid (Free)

American College Testing Program
P.O. Box 168
Iowa City, IA 52243
(319) 337-1040

The College Cost Book, **Item #004329 ($15.00 plus shipping and handling) This reference book is available in most libraries and high school guidance counselors' offices.**

> College Board Publications
> Two College Way
> P.O. Box 1100
> Forrester Center, WV 25438-4100
> (800) 323-7155

Don't Miss Out ($6.00 plus shipping and handling) This financial aid book is available in most libraries and high school guidance counselors' offices.

The A's and B's of Academic Scholarships ($6.00 plus shipping and handling)

Earn and Learn ($4.00 plus shipping and handling) This publication lists co-operative jobs offered by federal agencies.

> Octameron Associates
> P.O. Box 2748
> Alexandria, VA 22301
> (703) 836-5480

Paying Less for College **($22.95) This handbook gives financial information on 1,700 colleges in the nation, including the percentage of need met at each school.**

> Petersons'
> Attention: Book Order Department
> P.O. Box 2123
> Princeton, NJ 08543
> (800) 338-3282

A Selected List of Fellowship Opportunities and Aids to Advanced Education, **NSF 88-119 (Free)**

> Publication Office
> National Science Foundation
> 1800 G Street, N.W.
> Room 527
> Washington, DC 20550

Student Loans:
> Student Loan Marketing Association (Sallie Mae)
> 1050 Thomas Jefferson Street, N.W.
> Washington, DC 20007
> (800) 831-5626
>
> New England Education Loan Marketing Corp. (Nellie Mae)
> 50 Braintree Hill Park, Suite 300
> Braintree, MA 02184
> (800) 634-9308

Scholarships and Grants:
> National Scholarship Research Service
> 2280 Airport Boulevard
> Santa Rosa, CA 95403
> (707) 546-6781
> (707) 545-5777 (24-hour Message Center)

child care
For a free copy of the brochure "Finding Good Child Care: A Checklist," contact:
> The Child Care Action Campaign
> 330 7th Avenue, 17th Floor
> New York, NY 10001
> (212) 239-0138

For child support help, *Handbook on Child Support Enforcement* (Free)
> National Reference Center, OCSE
> 370 L'Enfant Promenade, S.W.
> Washington, DC 20447

collectors and collectibles
Collectibles for Cash:
> *Where to Send It Directory* ($5.95 plus $1 postage)
> Pilot Books
> 103 Cooper Street
> Babylon, NY 11702

Collector Editions, a magazine for subscription
170 Fifth Avenue
New York, NY 10010
(212) 989-8700

Collectors Mart Magazine
P.O. Box 12830
Wichita, KS 67277

Tabloid, *Antique Trader Weekly*
P.O. Box 1050
Dubuque, IA 52004
(319) 588-2073

Collectors News
P.O. Box 156
Grundy Center, IA 50638
(319) 824-6981

miscellaneous brochures

"Catalog of Services and Publications in Standard & Poor's," Standard & Poor's (Free)
Public Relations Department
Standard & Poor's
25 Broadway
New York, NY 10004
(800) 221-5277

"The College Money Guide" (Free)
Octameron Associates
P.O. Box 2748
Alexandria, VA 22301
(703) 836-5480

"The Consumer Guide to Comprehensive Financial Planning," International Association for Financial Planning (Free)

"Financial Strategies for New Parents," International Association for Financial Planning (Free)

> International Association for Financial Planning
> Two Concourse Parkway
> Suite 800
> Atlanta, GA 30328
> (404) 395-1605
> (800) 945-4237

"Facts About Financial Planners," by the U.S. Federal Trade Commission. Cost: 50 cents.

> Consumer Information Center-3B
> P.O. Box 100
> Pueblo, CO 81002

toll-free helplines
ADOPTION

> Adoptive Families of America
> 1-800-372-3300
> Concerned United Birthparents
> 1-800-822-2777
> National Adoption Center
> 1-800-TO-ADOPT

CAMERAS

> Kodak (FunSaver "35")
> 1-800-242-2424
> 3M (Scotch)
> 1-800-695-3456

CARS

> Automobile Consumer Services   1-800-223-4882
> *Consumer Reports*
> Nationwide Autobrokers   1-800-521-7257
> New Car Price Service   1-800-933-5555

CRIME
We Tip Hotlines   1-800-78-CRIME

ELDERLY
Eldercare Locator Information   1-800-677-1116
Hospice Education Institute   1-800-331-1620
National Hospice Organization   1-800-658-8898
National Institute on Aging   1-800-222-2225

END OF LIFE
Choice in Dying   1-800-989-9455

ENVIRONMENT
American Public Information on the Environment
1-800-320-APIE
U.S. Environmental Protection Agency—Safe Drinking Water
1-800-426-4791

FAMILY CRISIS
Boys Town National Hotline   1-800-448-3000
Child Abuse Hotline   1-800-4-A-CHILD
Childhelp IOF Foresters
Covenant House   1-800-999-9999

FINANCES
Buying a Home—Fannie Mae   1-800-7-FANNIE
Credit Counseling Service
Debt Management—Consumer
National Referral Line   1-800-388-2227

FINANCES–CREDIT REPORTS ($8 PER INDIVIDUAL; $16 JOINT)
Equifax   1-800-685-1111
Experience Credit Data   1-800-682-7654
Trans Union   1-800-851-2674

FOOD

American Dietetic Association   1-800-366-1655
FDA Seafood Hotline   1-800-FDA-4010
USDA Meat and Poultry   1-800-535-4555

HEALTH AND ILLNESS

Alzheimer's Association   1-800-272-3900
American Cancer Society   1-800-ACS-2345
American Diabetes Association   1-800-DIABETES
American Heart Association   1-800-AHA-USA-1
Arthritis Foundation   1-800-283-7800
Asthma and Allergy Foundation   1-800-727-8462
Centers for Disease Control—HIV and AIDS   1-800-342-AIDS
Certification Verification—American Board of Medical
    Specialties   1-800-776-CERT
Cystic Fibrosis Foundation   1-800-FIGHT-CF
Epilepsy Foundation   1-800-EFA-1000
National Cancer Institute   1-800-4-CANCER
National Clearinghouse for Alcohol and Drug Information
    1-800-729-6686
National Headache Foundation   1-800-843-2256
National Heart, Lung, and Blood Institute—High Blood Pressure
    1-800-575-WELL
National Institute of Mental Health   1-800-421-4211
National Mental Health Association   1-800-969-6642
National Multiple Sclerosis Society   1-800-FIGHT-MS
Prevent Blindness America   1-800-331-2020
Y-Me National Breast Cancer   1-800-221-2141

MISSING CHILDREN

Missing Children Help Center   1-800-USA-KIDS
National Center for Missing and Exploited Children
    1-800-THE-LOST
Vanished Children's Alliance   1-800-826-4743

PARENTS/PARENTING

American Sudden Infant Death Syndrome   1-800-232-SIDS
ASPO/Lamaze Information   1-800-368-4404
Breast-feeding/La Leche League   1-800-LA-LECHE
Child Abuse   1-800-422-4453
Childbirth—Depression After Delivery   1-800-944-4773
Fisher-Price Toys   1-800-432-5437
Gerber   1-800-4-GERBER
Immunization Information   1-800-232-2522
Mattel   1-800-524-8697
National Center for Stuttering   1-800-221-2483
Nintendo Help   1-800-255-3700
Nutrition—Beechnut Nutrition   1-800-523-6633
Playskool   1-800-752-9755
Tyco   1-800-367-8926

PETS

In Defense of Animals Stolen
Pet Hotline   1-800-STOLEN-PET
Petfinders   1-800-666-5678

RETIREMENT

American Association of Retired Persons   1-800-424-2277
Estimate Request Application   1-800-772-1213
Social Security Earnings/Benefit

SAFETY

Consumer Product Safety Commission   1-800-638-2772
National Highway Traffic Administration Auto Safety
    1-800-424-9393
National Safety Council   1-800-621-6244
SafetyBelt Safety USA   1-800-745-SAFE

TRAVEL

American Airlines 1-800-433-7300
Amtrak 1-800-USA-RAIL
Best Western International 1-800-528-1234
Continental Airlines 1-800-525-0280
Delta Airlines 1-800-221-1212
Greyhound 1-800-231-2222
Holiday Inn Worldwide 1-800-465-4329
Howard Johnson 1-800-654-2000
Northwest Airlines 1-800-225-2525
Ramada Worldwide 1-800-228-2828
Red Roof Inns 1-800-874-9000
Trans World Airlines 1-800-221-2000
Travelodge 1-800-255-3050
United Airlines 1-800-241-6522
USAirways 1-800-428-4322

VOTING

League of Women Voters 1-800-249-VOTE
Project Vote Smart 1-800-622-SMART

WASHING MACHINES

Admiral 1-800-688-9920
Amana 1-800-843-0304
Asko 1-800-367-2444
Frigidaire 1-800-451-7007
General Electric 1-800-626-2000
Hotpoint 1-800-626-2000
KitchenAid 1-800-422-1230
Magic Chef 1-800-688-1120
Maytag 1-800-688-9900
Roper 1-800-447-6737
Sears Contact local Sears store
Whirlpool 1-800-253-1301
White–Westinghouse 1-800-245-0600

WATER RELATED NUMBERS (SOME ARE NOT TOLL-FREE)

Low-Flush Toilets

American Standard   1-800-524-9797

Briggs   1-800-888-4458

Crane   1-800-877-6678

Eljer   1-972-407-2600

Kohler   1-414-457-4441

Mansfield   1-419-938-5211

Mister Miser   1-217-228-6900

Peerless Pottery   1-800-457-5785

Toto Kiki   1-714-282-8686

Universal-Rundle   1-800-955-0316

Low-Flow Showerheads

Alsons   1-800-421-0001

Chatham   1-800-526-7553

Interbath (8 a.m.–5 p.m. Pacific)   1-800-800-2132

Kohler   1-414-457-4441

Melard   1-800-635-2731

Moen   1-800-553-6636

Resources Conservation   1-800-243-2862

Scald Safe   1-203-964-0600

Speakman   1-302-764-9100

Teledyne Water Pik   1-800-525-2774

Whedon   1-800-541-2184

The following *freebie* information is important—the Consumer Information Catalog! Here is a list of more than 200 booklets filled with priceless information on topics such as cars, children, parenting, employment, environment, government programs, food, benefits, medical problems, housing tips, home improvements, money problems, credit problems, financial planning, small business, travel, hobbies, human rights, and assistance programs. Most booklets are free, some are 50 cents to $2.00—write to this address and ask for a CIC (Consumer Information Catalog).

Catalog Department
Consumer Information Center-6D
P.O. Box 100
Pueblo, CO 81002

. . . or fax this request to (719) 948-9724

. . . or use the Internet at http://www.peublo.gsa.gov

final free fact

Run to your library for a wealth of *free* information you didn't know existed! Everything on colleges, consumer reports, financial aid and grants, jobs and their ratings plus where to look. You'll be amazed!

organize your
life

time and
organization
sheets

We're organization nuts because we've learned that organization pays! See for yourself: The better organized you are, the smoother your life is—and the better you can keep track of your money.

We've collected organization ideas over the years, and have come up with some one-page sheets of guidelines that help us stay on track in all aspects of our lives. Use them to *organize your* L-I-F-E in the following ways:

L   Lots of things around the house
I   It's your money—make the most of it
F   Facts of life (births, marriage, death)
E   Events to look forward to

As a special bonus, we also offer our "Business in a Box," because we all know that sometimes stretching your money isn't as effective as making *more*.

We use these sheets over and over again, and invite you to do the same. We hope they help you, too!

life

Lots of things around the house

WEEKLY HOME MAINTENANCE

GENERAL

Carpets—vacuum, including stairs
Hardwood floors—wash with water
Windowsills—wipe clean
Baseboards—dust
Wastebaskets—empty
Furniture—dust
Glass tables—polish
Mini-blinds—dust

KITCHEN

Kitchen grill—(when used) clean (no abrasives)
Stove, countertops, sink, refrigerator top & sides,
small appliances—clean & polish
Microwave interior—clean (no abrasives)

LIVING ROOM/TV ROOM/DINING ROOM

Fireplace glass doors—clean both sides
Hearth—damp mop
Mantel—wipe clean

BATHS

Floor—wash with cleaning solvent
Tub, sink, toilet—scrub & polish
Mirror—polish
Towels—straighten

BEDROOMS

Beds—change sheets, square corners; side & top even

BASEMENT (PLAYROOM)

Appliances, folding table—wipe clean (move items on top)

FRONT PORCH (OUTSIDE)

Floor—sweep

LIVING AND BEDROOMS
1. Look up for cobwebs.
2. Dust windowsills and tops.
   Dust top of door frame.
3. Dust mirrors, pictures on wall.
4. Empty ashtrays.
5. Empty wastebaskets & reline.
6. Change linens.
7. Dust lamps and shades.
8. Polish furniture.
9. Vacuum under bed.

KITCHEN
1. Clean top of refrigerator.
2. Clean range hood.
3. Look up for cobwebs.
4. Clean cabinet doors.
5. Clean stove top.
6. Clean exterior of all
   appliances.
7. Dust windowsills and
   frames.
8. Dust pictures.
9. Dust top of door frames.
10. Clean backsplash and
    countertop.
11. Clean sink.

BATHS
1. Look for cobwebs.
2. Clean tile area
   behind tub.
3. Clean tub.
4. Polish chrome.
5. Clean shower door.
6. Clean toilet—inside
   and out.
7. Clean mirror and
   tile edge.
8. Clean bowl.
9. Clean countertop.

YOU'RE DONE!! NOW GO PLAY!!!

SPEEDY SHOPPER

ITEMS	AISLE	ITEMS	AISLE	ITEMS	AISLE
Air Freshners	____	Dinners, Box/Can	____	Nuts	____
Aluminum Foils	____	Dish Soap	____	Oatmeal	____
Applesauce	____	Drinks, Powdered	____	Oils	____
Aspirins	____	Dog Food	____	Pancake Mix	____
Automotive	____	Eggs	____	Paper Plates	____
Baby Food	____	Evap/Dry Milk	____	Paper Towels	____
Baby Formula	____	Fabric Softener	____	Parmesan Cheese	____
Barley	____	Facial Tissue	____	Pasta	____
Bar Soap	____	Feminine	____	Peanut Butter	____
Bath Tissue	____	Film	____	Pet Supplies	____
Batteries	____	First Aid	____	Pickles/Olives	____
BBQ Sauce	____	Fish, Canned	____	Pie Filling	____
Beans, Dry	____	Flour	____	Pizza, Boxed	____
Beer	____	Frozen Food	____	Popcorn	____
Birdseed	____	Fruits, Canned	____	Potatoes, Can/Box	____
Bleach	____	Fruits, Dried	____	Raisins	____
Bread	____	Furniture Polish	____	Relish	____
Breadcrumbs	____	Gelatin	____	Rice	____
Breading	____	Greeting Cards	____	Salad Dressing	____
Breakfast Food	____	Grits/Meal	____	Salt	____
Brooms & Mops	____	Health/Beauty	____	Sauces—Steak, etc.	____
Cake Frosting	____	Honey	____	Seltzer	____
Cake Mix	____	Hosiery	____	Shoe Polish	____
Candy	____	Ice	____	Soft Drinks	____
Cat Food	____	Ice Cream	____	Soup	____
Catsup	____	Insecticides	____	Spaghetti Sauces	____
Cereal	____	Instant Potatoes	____	Spice/Gravy	____
Charcoal	____	Jams & Jellies	____	Sponges	____
Cherries	____	Juices	____	Stationery	____
Chips, Potato	____	Kosher	____	Straws	____
Cleaners	____	Light Bulbs	____	Stuffing	____
Coffee	____	Lunch Bags	____	Sugar	____
Cookies	____	Marinade	____	Tea	____
Crackers	____	Marshmallows	____	Tobacco	____
Croutons	____	Mayonnaise	____	Toppings/Cones	____
Cupcakes	____	Matches	____	Toothpicks	____
Cupcake Papers	____	Meats, Canned	____	Trash Bags	____
Deodorant	____	Mexican/Chinese	____	Vegetables, Can	____
Desserts	____	Morsels	____	Velveeta	____
Detergents	____	Milk, Dry	____	Vinegar	____
Diapers	____	Mushrooms	____	Vitamins	____
Diet Foods	____	Mustard	____	Water	____
				Wine	____
				Other:	____

DIRECTIONS:
1. Copy many copies of this list onto white paper first!
2. Go to your favorite grocery store and fill in aisle numbers.
3. Highlight all aisle #1 items that you need in one color, aisle #2 items another color, etc. (If this is too much trouble for you, this list will still help you be a speedier shopper at a glance. Circle items needed on your list.)

OTHER ERRANDS:

QUICK CLEANING

LIVING ROOM

- [ ] Clear clutter
- [ ] Clean glass, mirrors, tabletops
- [ ] Dust furniture, lamps, windowsills, pictures
- [ ] Empty wastebaskets
- [ ] Vacuum carpets, damp-mop floors

BEDROOMS

- [ ] Clear clutter
- [ ] Straighten closet and hang up clothes
- [ ] Sort laundry for mending and dry cleaning
- [ ] Change linens
- [ ] Clean mirrors, glass, tabletops
- [ ] Dust furniture, windowsills, pictures
- [ ] Empty wastebaskets
- [ ] Vacuum or dust-mop floors/carpet

BATHROOMS

- [ ] Clear clutter
- [ ] Collect dirty towels and take to laundry area
- [ ] Spray and wipe mirror with glass cleaner
- [ ] Clean sink
- [ ] Use glass cleaner on faucets and chrome
- [ ] Spray tub/shower walls with heavy-duty cleaner
- [ ] Squirt cleaner in toilet bowl and swish around bowl
- [ ] Wipe outside of bowl
- [ ] Wipe off windowsills and scale
- [ ] Empty wastebaskets
- [ ] Vacuum carpets, damp-mop floor

KITCHEN

- [ ] Organize clutter, including drawers
- [ ] Clean countertops
- [ ] Clean outside of large appliances with glass cleaner
- [ ] Shine outside of small appliances with glass cleaner
- [ ] Clean inside toaster oven, toaster, and microwave
- [ ] Wipe off windowsills
- [ ] Wash and disinfect trash can, replace lliner
- [ ] Sweep or vacuum floor, then damp-mop

BIGGER JOBS: ROTATE

- [ ] Polish wood furniture
- [ ] Use attachments to vacuum baseboards, moldings, lampshades, and behind furniture
- [ ] Vacuum furniture and drapes
- [ ] Recycle magazines and newspapers
- [ ] Dust knickknacks, polish silver
- [ ] Clean inside cabinets and drawers
- [ ] Wash small rugs
- [ ] Scrub tile and grout
- [ ] Clean baseboards and woodwork
- [ ] Clean inside of medicine cabinet
- [ ] Wash shower curtain
- [ ] Scrub floor
- [ ] Clean range top thoroughly and replace burner bibs; vacuum vents
- [ ] Clean oven
- [ ] Clean woodwork
- [ ] Clean out pantry, cabinets, and drawers
- [ ] Scrub and wax floor

"STUFF" STORAGE

		GARAGE	ATTIC	BASEMENT	SHED	OTHER
HOUSEHOLD STUFF	Carpenter tools					
	Costumes					
	Extension cords					
	Extra house and/ or car key					
	Fire extinguisher					
	Garden tools					
	Holiday decorations					
	Lawn furniture					
	Power tools					
	Snow shovels/Ice pick					
	Wrapping paper/ Ribbons					
	Miscellaneous					
SPORTS STUFF	Baseball stuff					
	Beach balls, etc.					
	Bowling balls					
	Camping gear					
	Fishing pole/Tackle box					
	Skates					
	Skiing gear					
	Sleds					
	Tennis stuff					
SEASONAL STUFF	Bathing suits					
	Beach towels					
	Boots/Galoshes					
	Coats/Raincoats					
	Hats/Gloves/Scarves					
PERSONAL STUFF	Bankbooks					
	Extra checks/ Checkbook					
	House deed or rental lease					
	Insurance policies					
	Mortgage/ Loan agreements					
	Photographs/ Photo albums					
	Safe deposit key					
	School records/ Military papers					
	Tax forms and information					
	Will					
	Yearbooks					

YARD SALE CHECKLIST

DO	✓	NOTES
1. Date set		
2. Ad placed in newspaper		
3. Signs made		
4. Signs posted		
5. Signs removed after garage sale		
6. Items for sale are assembled in one place		
7. Label areas		
8. Before sale:		
Price items		
Set up tables		
Items in categories and displayed		
Plug available for testing of appliances		
Individual sales account sheet		
Other		
9. Sale day:		
Get up early		
Post signs		
Move out tables		
"Money box" handler		
Sell and record on account sheet		
Place all remaining items in boxes for charity		
Clean up		
Remove signs from neighborhood		

ACCOUNT PAGE

NAME	NAME	NAME	NAME	NAME	NAME	NAME
2.50	1.50	.25	.50	2.00	1.50	1.00
.75	1.00	1.00	2.50	11.50	1.00	1.50
1.00	1.50	1.50	1.00	.50	1.00	1.50
						1.50

TOTALS

4.25	4.00	2.75	4.00	14.00	3.50	5.50

life

It's your money— make the most of it

"SIMPLE" GETTING-ORGANIZED CHECKLIST

LAWYER

- ☐ Last will (the original)
- ☐ Living will
- ☐ Power of attorney
- ☐ Medical power of attorney
- ☐ Safe-deposit key
- ☐ Instructions on burial plots

SAFE-DEPOSIT BOX

- ☐ Birth certificates
- ☐ Death certificates
- ☐ Marriage certificates
- ☐ Divorce decree
- ☐ Last will (copy)
- ☐ Passports
- ☐ Military service records
- ☐ Veterans Administration papers
- ☐ Adoption papers
- ☐ Social Security papers
- ☐ Letters of instruction (copy)
- ☐ Power of attorney (copy)
- ☐ Stock certificates or bonds
- ☐ Car titles
- ☐ Deeds
- ☐ Contracts/IOUs
- ☐ Household inventories
- ☐ Home records
- ☐ Insurance policies (copies)
- ☐ Retirement/pension plan papers

AT-HOME FILES

- ☐ Sheet for location of important papers
- ☐ Sheet for personal information
- ☐ Sheet for your immunizations
- ☐ Job records

- ☐ Education papers
- ☐ Degrees or certificates
- ☐ Medical records
- ☐ Birth certificates (copy)
- ☐ Death certificates (copy)
- ☐ Family medical records
- ☐ Cemetery records

FINANCIAL FILE

- ☐ Unpaid bills
- ☐ Bank statements
- ☐ Canceled checks (5 years)
- ☐ Credit card information
- ☐ Insurance policies (originals)
  - **Auto**
  - **Disability**
  - **Homeowner's**
  - **Life**
  - **Medical**
  - **Other**
- ☐ Mortgage information
- ☐ Loan information
- ☐ Manuals and warranties (including dates and places of purchase)
- ☐ Home-improvement records
- ☐ Tax receipts
- ☐ Tax returns (5 years)

STORAGE BOX

- ☐ Tax returns (more than 5 years old)
- ☐ Family health records
- ☐ Canceled checks (important debts only after 5 years)
- ☐ Receipts of major debts
- ☐ Home-improvement records

ORGANIZING YOUR PERSONAL RECORDS

A. SAFE-DEPOSIT BOX
1. Birth certificates
2. Death certificates
3. Marriage certificate
4. Veteran's papers
5. Social Security papers
6. Bonds and stock
7. Deeds
8. Automobile titles
9. Household inventory
10. Home records (blueprints, deeds, surveys)
11. Contracts of any type
12. Insurance policies
13. IOUs
14. Retirement and pension-plan documents
15. Wills or trusts
16. Instructions in case of death
17. Guardianship assignment

B. AT HOME
1. Unpaid bills
2. Current bank statements
3. Current canceled checks and money-order receipts
4. Credit card numbers
5. Loan papers and payment books
6. Warranties (including dates and places of purchase)
7. Insurance policies:
     Home
     Life
     Automobile
     Health and medical
8. Employment records
9. Health benefits information
10. Family health records
11. Will copies
12. Death instructions
13. Education papers

14. Important telephone numbers
15. Place of spare key to safe-deposit box
16. Receipts for warranty items
17. Tax receipts
18. All paid-bill receipts
19. Income tax working papers
20. Credit papers and statements
21. Medical, dental, and drug expenses
22. Records of business expenses for taxes and budget

C. STORE PERMANENTLY IN HOUSE
1. Old tax returns
2. Home improvement records
3. Proof of payment for major debts
4. Old canceled checks

YOUR NET WORTH

NAME: _____ **DATE:** _____

Assets (Included in your will)

Cash on hand
Individual checking account
Individual savings account
Certificates of deposit
IOUs
Life Insurance to the estate
Share of business
Automobiles
Household furnishings
Arts and antiques
Jewelry and furs
Other valuables, holdings, etc.
TOTAL:

Assets (Passed on outside your will)

Joint checking account
Joint savings account
Joint owned property
Trusts
Life insurance to a specific beneficiary
Individual retirement accounts
Pension or retirement benefits
TOTAL:

Debts

Mortage balance
Loan balance
Charge account balances
Credit card balances
Miscellaneous bills
Past taxes owed
TOTAL:

Total assets included in your will
   PLUS   +
Total assets passed outside your will
   LESS   −
Total debts
   EQUALS   =
NET WORTH:

MONTHLY INCOME AND EXPENSES

INCOME PER MONTH _____
Salary _____
Interest _____
Dividends _____
Notes _____
Rents _____

TOTAL GROSS INCOME _____

LESS
1. Tithe _____
2. Tax _____

NET SPENDING INCOME _____

3. Housing _____
Mortgage (rent) _____
Insurance _____
Taxes _____
Electricity _____
Gas _____
Water _____
Sanitation _____
Telephone _____
Maintenance _____
Other _____

4. Food _____

5. Automobile(s) _____
Payments _____
Gas & Oil _____
Insurance _____
License _____
Taxes _____
Maint./Repair/
  Replacement _____

6. Insurance _____
Life _____
Medical _____
Other _____

7. Debts _____
Credit Card _____
Loans & Notes _____
Other _____

8. Enter. & Recreation _____
Eating Out _____
Trips _____
Baby-sitters _____
Activities _____
Vacation _____
Other _____

9. Clothing _____

10. Savings _____

11. Medical Expenses _____
Doctor _____
Dentist _____
Drugs _____
Other _____

12. Miscellaneous _____
Toiletry, cosmetics _____
Beauty, barber _____
Laundry, cleaning _____
Allowances,
  lunches _____
Subscriptions _____
Gifts
  (incl. Christmas) _____
Special Education _____
Cash _____
Other _____

TOTAL EXPENSES _____

INCOME VS. EXPENSE
Net Spendable Income _____

Less Expenses _____

MONTHLY INCOME AND EXPENSES

YEARLY INCOME (GROSS) _____

MONTHLY INCOME (GROSS) _____

LESS
Tax _____

NET INCOME _____

1. Housing (30%)
Mortgage (rent) _____
Insurance _____
Taxes _____
Electricity _____
Gas _____
Water _____
Sanitation _____ Total
Telephone _____
Maintenance _____
Other _____

2. Food (17%)
_____
Total

3. Auto (15%)
Payments _____
Gas & Oil _____
Insurance _____ _____
License _____ Total
Taxes _____
Maint./Repair/
 Replacement _____

4. Insurance (5%)
Life _____
Medical _____ _____
Other _____ Total

5. Debts (5%)
Credit Cards _____
Loans & Notes _____ _____
Other _____ Total

6. Enter. & Recreation (7%)
Eating Out _____
Trips _____
Baby-sitters _____ _____
Activities _____ Total
Vacation _____

7. Clothing (5%)
_____
Total

8. Savings (5%) _____ _____
Total

9. Medical Expenses (5%)
Doctor _____
Dental _____ _____
Drugs _____ Total
Other _____

10. Miscellaneous (6%)
Toiletry, cosmet. _____
Beauty, barber _____
Laundry, cleaning _____
Allow., lunches _____
Subscriptions _____ _____
Gifts _____ Total
Special Education _____
Cash _____
Other _____

TOTAL EXPENSES
(#1–10 Totals) _____

Net Income _____

Surplus
(Income – Expenses) _____

"QUICKIE" BUDGET

A.

INCOME

Husband's take-home pay	_____	Gas and electricity	_____
Wife's take-home pay	_____	Water	_____
Other income	_____	Garbage	_____
Dividends	_____	Telephone	_____
Interest	_____	Food	_____
Other money (profit-sharing,		Transportation	_____
pension, royalties, trust, etc.)	_____	Child care	_____
		Medical/dental	_____
TOTAL (A)	_____	Education	_____
		Debts or loans	
		(car payments, etc.)	_____

B.

EXPENSES

Housing (rent or mortgage)	_____	Personal expenses	_____
Taxes, income (if not withheld)	_____	Drug items	_____
Taxes, property (money		Clothing	_____
set aside for annual		Home maintenance & furnishing	_____
payments)	_____	Entertainment/recreation	_____
Insurance	_____	Domestic help	_____
Auto	_____	Charitable donations	_____
Disability	_____	Vacation savings	_____
Health	_____	Holiday expenses/gifts	_____
Life	_____	Other	_____
Utilities	_____		_____
		TOTAL (B)	_____
		A – B = Leftover for savings	_____

"QUICKIE" DEBT LIST

Creditor	Reason for Loan	Monthly Payment	Total Amount Owed
	Total Monthly Payments	$	$
		Total Amount Owed	$

Loan Payments as a percentage of Income = $\dfrac{\text{Total Monthly Payments}}{\text{Net Monthly Income}} = \dfrac{\$ \underline{\hspace{1cm}}}{\$ \underline{\hspace{1cm}}} = \underline{\hspace{1cm}}\%$

Total loan payments, except mortgage, should not exceed 20% of net income.

SIMPLE BUDGET

INCOME
  1. Net salary   _____
  2. Interest, dividends, bonuses   _____
  3. Alimony, child support receive   _____
  4. Pension   _____
  5. Social Security   _____
  6. Gifts   _____
  7. Other income   _____

                        _____
                        _____

Total cash receipts   _____

EXPENSES
  1. Rent/Mortgage   _____
  2. Food   _____
  3. Household maintenance   _____
  4. Utilities and telephone   _____
  5. Clothing   _____
  6. Personal expenses   _____
  7. Medical and dental care   _____
  8. Automobile/Transportation
      costs   _____
  9. Child care expenses   _____
10. Entertainment   _____
11. Vacation(s)   _____
12. Gifts   _____
13. Insurance   _____
14. Real estate taxes   _____
15. Loan payments   _____
16. Credit card payments   _____
17. Alimony/Child support
      payments   _____
18. Tuition/
      Educational expenses   _____
19. Savings   _____
20. Other expense   _____

                        _____
                        _____

Total expenses   _____
Surplus   _____

DETAILED BUDGET

Budget for the month of _____

EXPENSES	BUDGETED AMOUNT	ACTUAL EXPENSE	EXPENSES	BUDGETED AMOUNT	ACTUAL EXPENSE
HOUSING			**CHILD SUPPLIES**		
rent or mortgage	_____	_____	toys and games	_____	_____
real estate taxes	_____	_____	lessons and instruction	_____	_____
homeowner's			diapers, etc.	_____	_____
insurance	_____	_____	extracurricular		
water	_____	_____	school fees	_____	_____
heat	_____	_____			
electricity	_____	_____	**AUTO**		
gas	_____	_____	loan payments	_____	_____
telephone	_____	_____	insurance	_____	_____
			maintenance	_____	_____
FOOD			repair	_____	_____
groceries	_____	_____	Gas and oil	_____	_____
restaurants	_____	_____			
			HOUSEHOLD EQUIPMENT		
CLOTHING/ SHOES			appliances	_____	_____
husband	_____	_____	furniture	_____	_____
wife	_____	_____	tools	_____	_____
child	_____	_____			
child	_____	_____	**TRANSPORTATION**		
			taxi	_____	_____
HOUSEHOLD/ YARD			carpool	_____	_____
laundry	_____	_____	parking	_____	_____
dry cleaning	_____	_____			
repair	_____	_____	**MISCELLANEOUS**		
housekeeping	_____	_____	newspapers	_____	_____
gardening	_____	_____	magazines	_____	_____
			organization dues	_____	_____
			toiletries	_____	_____
MEDICAL			hobby supplies	_____	_____
doctor	_____	_____	music	_____	_____
dentist	_____	_____	books	_____	_____
prescriptions	_____	_____	other	_____	_____
over-the-counter drugs	_____	_____			
insurance payments	_____	_____	**ENTERTAINMENT**		
			movies	_____	_____
CHILD CARE			travel	_____	_____
day care	_____	_____			
baby-sitters	_____	_____	**GIFTS**		
				_____	_____
				_____	_____
			OTHER		
				_____	_____
				_____	_____

SAVINGS FORMULAS
(7% INTEREST COMPOUNDED MONTHLY)

TO SAVE $25,000 . . .
in 1 year you need to save $2,017 a month
in 5 years you need to save $349 a month
in 10 years you need to save $144 a month
in 15 years you need to save $79 a month
in 16 years you need to save $71 a month
in 17 years you need to save $64 a month
in 18 years you need to save $58 a month

TO SAVE $50,000 . . .
in 1 year you need to save $4,035 a month
in 5 years you need to save $698 a month
in 10 years you need to save $289 a month
in 15 years you need to save $158 a month
in 16 years you need to save $142 a month
in 17 years you need to save $128 a month
in 18 years you need to save $116 a month

TO SAVE $75,000 . . .
in 1 year you need to save $6,052 a month
in 5 years you need to save $1,048 a month
in 10 years you need to save $433 a month
in 15 years you need to save $237 a month
in 16 years you need to save $213 a month
in 17 years you need to save $192 a month
in 18 years you need to save $174 a month

Note: To save larger amounts, in increments of $25,000, multiply the monthly amount listed by the appropriate factor. For example, to save $100,000 in 18 years, double the amount listed for $50,000 ($116 x 2 = $232 a month)

IF YOU SAVE $100 PER MONTH . . .

Interest Rate	5 years	10 years	15 years	20 years	25 years	30 years	35 years	40 years
5	$6,829	$15,593	$26,840	$41,275	$59,799	$83,573	$114,083	$153,238
5½	6,920	16,024	28,002	43,762	64,498	91,780	127,675	174,902
6	7,012	16,470	29,227	46,435	69,646	100,954	143,183	200,599
6½	7,106	16,932	30,519	49,308	75,289	111,217	160,898	229,599
7	7,201	17,409	31,881	52,397	81,480	122,709	181,156	264,012
7½	7,298	17,904	33,318	55,719	88,274	135,587	204,345	304,272
8	7,397	18,417	34,835	59,295	95,737	150,030	230,918	351,428
8½	7,497	18,947	36,435	63,144	103,937	166,240	261,395	406,726
9	7,599	19,497	38,124	67,290	112,953	184,447	296,385	471,643
9½	7,703	20,066	39,908	71,756	122,872	204,913	336,590	547,933
10	7,808	20,655	41,792	76,570	133,789	227,933	382,828	637,678

SAMPLE BUDGET PERCENTAGES AND DOLLAR AMOUNTS

	*NSI	Percentage		Amount
Housing (Total)	$1,500 ×	30	=	$450
Food	1,500 ×	16	=	240
Auto (Total)	1,500 ×	15	=	225
Insurance	1,500 ×	5	=	75
Debts	1,500 ×	5	=	75
Entertainment	1,500 ×	7	=	105
Clothing	1,500 ×	5	=	75
Savings	1,500 ×	5	=	75
Medical Expenses	1,500 ×	5	=	75
Miscellaneous	1,500 ×	7	=	105
TOTALS		100		$1,500

*NSI = net spendable income

SAMPLE BUDGET PERCENTAGES

	Percentages
Housing (Total)	30–36
Food	12–17
Auto (Total)	15–20
Insurance	3–7
Debts	5–6
Entertainment	5–8
Clothing	5–6
Savings	5
Medical Expenses	4–8
Miscellaneous	5–10

LIST OF DEBTS

To Whom Owed	Contact Name Phone Number	Payoff	Payments Left	Monthly Payment	Date

*PAYMENT PER $1,000 OF LOAN

Interest Rate (Percent)	15 Years	30 Years
7.00	$8.99	$6.66
7.25	9.13	6.83
7.50	9.28	7.00
7.75	9.42	7.17
8.00	9.56	7.34
8.25	9.71	7.52
8.50	9.85	7.69
8.75	10.00	7.87
9.00	10.15	8.05
9.25	10.30	8.23

*For a loan of $60,000 for 15 years at 8% interest, multiply 60 × $9.56 to see your monthly payments ($573.60 mo.).

Loan Amount	Monthly Payment (Approximate)	Total *Interest
$100	$3	$19.52
200	7	39.04
300	10	58.56
400	13	78.44
500	17	97.96
1,000	33	195.56
2,000	66	391.48
3,000	100	587.04
4,000	133	782.96
5,000	166	978.52
6,000	199	1,174.44
7,000	232	1,370.00
8,000	266	1,565.56
9,000	299	1,761.48
10,000	332	1,957.04

*Calculates 12% interest (APR) over 3 years.

COLLEGE BUDGET

FIRST SEMESTER Expense			SECOND SEMESTER	
	Budget	Actual	Budget	Actual
Tuition	$	$	$	$
Fees				
Room				
Meals				
Books				
Equipment & supplies				
Lab fees				
Travel to & from school				
All other travel				
Recreation/entertainment				
Clothing				
Laundry				
Grooming				
Health expenditures				
Automobile insurance				
Snacks				
Major expenses (car, etc.)				
Miscellaneous costs				
TOTAL	$	$	$	$

FOUR-YEAR COLLEGE, INCLUDING ROOM AND BOARD

Year Entering	Public College or University	Private College or University
1993	$27,400	$69,800
1994	29,592	73,385
1995	31,959	81,415
1996	34,500	87,928
1997	37,277	94,962
1998	40,260	102,559
1999	43,380	110,764
2000	46,959	119,625
2001	50,715	129,195
2002	54,773	139,530
2003	59,155	150,693
2004	63,887	162,748
2005	68,998	175,768
2006	74,518	189,830
2007	80,480	205,016
2008	86,917	221,417
2009	93,871	239,130
2010	101,380	258,260
2011	109,490	278,922
2012	118,250	301,236
2013	127,710	325,335
2014	137,927	351,362
2015	148,960	379,470

COLLEGE FINANCIAL AID

Pell Grants

Grants of $200 to $2,100 per year, based on financial need, not academic achievement. If a student qualifies, he or she automatically receives the money. The student must apply for this grant before he or she can be considered for other federal aid. The student applies for the grant by filling out the federal government's Free Application for Student Federal Aid (FASFA). Check with the college office.

Supplemental Educational Opportunity Grants

Grants of from $200 to $4,000 per year, based on need. SEOG is a federal program that supplements Pell grants. Under this program, funds are awarded directly to colleges, which in turn dispense the money. They are intended for families with the lowest incomes. To apply, a student should request information directly from the financial aid offices of the college he or she will attend.

Perkins Loan

Low-interest loans to students based on need. The amount available varies with the program: up to $4,500 for students in vocational programs who have completed less than two years of study toward a bachelor's degree, $9,600 for undergraduates who already have completed two years of study, and $18,000 for graduate and professional students. The amount of aid any individual student receives depends on financial need, other aid received, and the availability of funds. It's entirely up to the school to decide how to divide the money; a Perkins loan is not an entitlement.

Stafford Loans

Federally insured and subsidized loans offered through private lenders. Loans of $2,625 available to undergraduates, $4,000 to upperclassmen, and $7,500 to graduate students each year.

College Work-Study Program

Minimum-wage or near-minimum-wage jobs for needy students; the programs are administered by each college or university.

The details of each program vary from year to year. For information on how to apply for federal aid, refer to "The Student Guide," a reference manual for federal government financial assistance, which is issued each year by the Department of Education. For a free copy, contact the Federal Student Aid Information Center, P.O. Box 84, Washington, DC; (800) 433-3243.

Facts of life (births, marriage, death)

BABY PLANNING

Before you even think about a baby!

☐ Review health insurance coverage *before* conception.

☐ If necessary, buy health insurance, paying special attention to the date when your pregnancy will be covered. (Could save you thousands!)

After Conception:
First Month

☐ Select a doctor.

Get recommendations.

Check credentials.

Interview prospective doctors or midwifes.

Find out where your prospective health-care professionals have staff privileges.

Make your selection.

☐ Decide where to have your baby: a hospital? a birthing center? at home?

☐ Visit the facilities if the location of where you would like to deliver plays a major role in determining who will deliver your baby.

☐ Select a facility.

☐ Again consult with the insurance company to clarify which specific procedures during pregnancy are covered.

Fourth Month

☐ Review the maternity/paternity policy at your workplace(s).

Fifth Month

☐ Plan your will.

Estimate your net worth.

Plan the distribution of your assets.

Make an appointment with an attorney.

Select an executor and get his or her approval.

☐ Select a guardian.

Select a guardian of the person and a guardian of the estate.

Make sure the guardian is willing to serve.

☐ Assess your life insurance needs.

Estimate the amount you will need.

Decide what kind of policy you will need.

Sixth Month

☐ Make your will.

Meet with an attorney.

Draft a power of attorney.

Draft a living will.

Write a letter of final instructions.

☐ Inform your guardian of your child-rearing wishes.

Write a letter of parental guidance.

☐ Evaluate life insurance options.

Collect estimates from four or five life insurance companies.

Seventh Month

☐ Execute your will.

Complete your will.

Store it in a safe place.

☐ Buy life insurance.

Purchase the best of policies you have reviewed.

Store the policy in a safe place.

☐ Prepare for your hospital stay.

Take childbirth classes.

Review your insurance coverage to make sure you understand the coverage and procedures.

Estimate your out-of-pocket health-care expenses.

☐ Prepare for the homecoming.

Arrange for child care for other children, if any.

Buy or borrow furniture and equipment.

Interview pediatricians. Ask other mothers.

Eighth Month

☐ Prepare for your hospital stay.

Preregister at the hospital.

Notify your insurance company and get a precertification number, if necessary.

Ninth Month

☐ Enjoy your last month of great sleep for a long, long while.

After Birth

☐ Get a birth certificate.

☐ Apply for a Social Security card.

☐ Add your child to insurance policies.

☐ Keep careful records of your health-care and other expenses.

☐ Obtain an itemized bill from the hospital.

☐ File health insurance claims.

☐ If necessary, select child care.
Decide on type of care.
Visit sites/interview candidates.
Select a facility/hire an individual.
If you hire an at-home worker, file the necessary paperwork for taxes, Social Security, unemployment, etc.

☐ Establish a new budget and make provisions for a college savings plan.

Yearly Duties

☐ Review your life insurance needs.
(Consider doing the review each time you write a check for your annual premiums.)

☐ Review your will. Have circumstances changed?

☐ Review your choice of guardian. Is your first choice still the best choice?

☐ Review your college savings budget.

CHILD IMMUNIZATION RECORD

Name: _____

Birth date: _____

Type of Shot	Dose #	Needed at:	Date Given
OPV (oral polio vaccine)	1	2 months	
	2	4 months	
	3	15 months	
	4	Before school	
DPT (diphtheria-pertussis-tetanus)	1	2 months	
	2	4 months	
	3	6 months	
	4	15 months	
	5	Before starting school	
	Adult Booster	Every 10 years (diphtheria and tetanus)	
MMR (measles-mumps-rubella)	1	15 months	
	2	Before starting school	
HIB (bacterial meningitis)	1	2 months	
	2	4 months	
	3	6 months	
	4	15 months	
HBV (hepatitis B virus)	1	At birth	
	2	1–2 months	
	3	6–18 months	

Notes: _____

WEDDING PLANNER

Twelve Months or More

☐ Choose location of ceremony

☐ Select reception site _____Phone _____

☐ Buy wedding rings, order engraving

Six to Twelve Months

☐ Order wedding gown

☐ Reserve limousine transportation

☐ Decide budget

☐ Decide type of wedding ☐*informal* ☐*formal*

☐ Compile bride and groom's invitation list _____No. Bride _____No. Groom

☐ Choose attendants

☐ Select veil and accessories

☐ Select attendants' gowns

☐ Select men's formal wear _____Phone _____

☐ Plan details of reception

☐ Select photographer _____Phone _____

☐ Select videographer _____Phone _____

☐ Select caterer _____Phone _____

☐ Select florist _____Phone _____

☐ Select bridal registry _____Phone _____

☐ Select music for wedding ceremony _____Phone _____

☐ Select music for reception _____Phone _____

☐ Discuss honeymoon plans

☐ Order wedding cake _____Phone _____

Four Months

☐ Make reservations for rehearsal dinner

☐ Order invitations, personal stationery, and wedding programs

☐ Shop for trousseau

☐ Find a new place to live

☐ Shop for home furnishings

☐ Set an appointment for complete physical exam

☐ Update your immunizations

☐ Set appointment for blood test (varies from state to state)

☐ Finalize honeymoon plans; travel agency

Three Months
- ☐ Address wedding invitations
- ☐ Select attendants' gifts
- ☐ Check local newspaper wedding announcement deadline
- ☐ Set a date with your fiancé to get your marriage license
(check state laws regarding length of validity)
- ☐ Reserve rental items for ceremony and reception

One Month
- ☐ Mail invitations
- ☐ Arrange for final fittings on your gown
- ☐ Remind bridesmaids of final gown fittings Date _____Time _____
- ☐ Test new hairstyles you're considering
- ☐ Buy groom's wedding gift
- ☐ Arrange lodging for out-of-town guests Phone _____
- ☐ Have formal wedding portrait taken Date _____Time _____
- ☐ Make reservations for bridemaids' luncheon
- ☐ Confirm honeymoon trip reservations/check luggage

Two Weeks
- ☐ Record wedding gifts as you receive them and write thank-you notes promptly
- ☐ Double-check attire and accessories for all members of the wedding party
- ☐ Confirm time & date of wedding rehearsal with members of the wedding party
- ☐ Review reception seating plans and prepare place cards, if necessary
- ☐ Arrange to move your belongings to your new home
- ☐ Schedule appointment with hairdresser & manicurist Date _____Time _____
- ☐ Arrange for name & address change on your bank account, credit cards, driver's license, etc.
- ☐ Complete trousseau shopping
- ☐ Arrange for a professional to preserve and heirloom your gown and florals

One Week
- ☐ Have final consultation with caterer, florist, musicians, and photographers
- ☐ Give final count to reception facility or caterer
- ☐ Host bridesmaids' luncheon Date _____Time _____
- ☐ Begin packing for honeymoon trip

BRIDE'S CHECKLIST

Wedding Stationery

- ☐ Invitations
- ☐ Announcements
- ☐ Reception Cards
- ☐ Respond Cards and Envelopes
- ☐ Respond Postcards
- ☐ Informals
- ☐ At-Home Cards
- ☐ Thank-You Scrolls
- ☐ Thank-You Notes
- ☐ Calligraphy Pens
- ☐ Wedding Programs
- ☐ Map Cards
- ☐ Pew Cards
- ☐ Calling Cards
- ☐ Photo Seals
- ☐ Bookmarks

Items for the Ceremony

- ☐ Aisle Runner
- ☐ Unity Candle
- ☐ Unity Candelabra
- ☐ Ring Bearer Pillow and Heart Tag
- ☐ Flower Girl Basket
- ☐ Taper Candles
- ☐ Bridal Purse
- ☐ Garters
- ☐ Pew Bows

Bridal Party Gifts

- ☐ Personalized Stationery
- ☐ Personalized Playing Cards
- ☐ Embroidered Gifts
- ☐ Personalized Glassware
- ☐ Appreciation Folders
- ☐ Personalized Accessories
- ☐ Specialty Gift Items

Books

- ☐ Thank-You Guide
- ☐ Wedding Pocket Book Planner
- ☐ Bridal Book
- ☐ Guest Book

Reception Items

- ☐ Beverage, Luncheon, Dinner Napkins
- ☐ Cake Boxes or Bags
- ☐ Book and Box Matches
- ☐ Matchbook Favor Notepads
- ☐ Favor-Making Necessities
- ☐ Cake Knife and Server
- ☐ Tissue Bell Decorations
- ☐ Colored Paper Plates and Cups
- ☐ Plastic Drinkware and Flatware
- ☐ Disposable Tableware
- ☐ Disposable Ashtrays
- ☐ Thank-You Ribbons and Scrolls
- ☐ Wishing Well Card Holder
- ☐ Colored Paper Streamers
- ☐ Just-Married Banners and Flags
- ☐ Keepsake/Keepcake Box
- ☐ Toasting Glasses
- ☐ Reception Aprons
- ☐ Place Cards
- ☐ Cake Top
- ☐ Table Covers
- ☐ Punch Cups
- ☐ Favor Ribbons
- ☐ Pencils
- ☐ Post-it Notes
- ☐ Plume Pen
- ☐ Candles
- ☐ Coasters
- ☐ Table Skirts
- ☐ Stir Sticks
- ☐ Balloons

OTHER WEDDING ITEMS

- ☐ Wedding File
- ☐ Bridal Gown Cover
- ☐ Personalized License Plate
- ☐ Wedding Service Video Case
- ☐ Marriage Certificate
- ☐ Car Decorating Kit
- ☐ Seeds of Love
- ☐ Bow Bag
- ☐ Gratuity Envelopes

PHOTOGRAPHY CHECKLIST

PHOTOGRAPHER _____

PHONE _____

BUDGETED COST _____

ACTUAL COST _____

FORMAL PORTRAITS–DATE & TIME _____

- ☐ Bride dressing for ceremony
- ☐ Bride, full-length solo
- ☐ Bride with parents
- ☐ Bride with mother & father separately
- ☐ Bride with grandparents
- ☐ Bride with sisters & brothers
- ☐ Bride with maid of honor
- ☐ Bride with attendants
- ☐ Bride with ring bearer, flower girl
- ☐ Garter being put on

- ☐ Groom, full-length solo
- ☐ Groom with parents
- ☐ Groom with mother & father separately
- ☐ Groom with grandparents
- ☐ Groom with sisters & brothers
- ☐ Groom with best man
- ☐ Groom with groomsmen

- ☐ Groom with bride's parents being seated for ceremony
- ☐ Bridesmaids walking down the aisle
- ☐ Flower girl, ring bearer walking down the aisle
- ☐ Bride and father approaching altar or canopy
- ☐ Bride's father giving her hand to groom
- ☐ Exchange of vows
- ☐ Ring ceremony
- ☐ Recessional

- ☐ Formal bride & groom together
- ☐ Newlyweds with parents
- ☐ Newlyweds with entire bridal party
- ☐ Close-ups of bride & groom's hands clasped together
- ☐ Receiving line-guests & bridal party

- ☐ Cake table
- ☐ Bride & groom cutting/feeding each other cake
- ☐ Best man toasting newlyweds
- ☐ Newlyweds toasting each other
- ☐ Cake & punch servers
- ☐ Musicians
- ☐ Newlyweds' first dance
- ☐ Guests dancing
- ☐ Bride tossing bouquet
- ☐ Groom removing garter
- ☐ Guests throwing rice
- ☐ Newlyweds getting into limo or car

- ☐ Postreception party
- ☐ Bride's mother assisting her into going-away outfit
- ☐ Bridegroom alone with new stepchildren

WEDDING BUDGET

Item	Budget	Actual
Bridal Gown & Accessories	$	$
Wedding Rings	$	$
Invitations	$	$
Rehearsal Dinner	$	$
Hall/Site Rental	$	$
Reception	$	$
Caterer	$	$
Music & Entertainment	$	$
Cake	$	$
Flowers	$	$
Photography	$	$
Videotography	$	$
Limousine	$	$
Attendants' Gifts	$	$
Clergy Fee	$	$
Other	$	$
Other	$	$
TOTAL	$	$

HONEYMOON CHECKLIST

Airfare	$
Ground transportation	$
Hotel or lodge	$
Food and beverage	$
Tips and gratuities	$
Sightseeing	$
Shopping	$
Total	$

Travel Agency _____ Phone _____

Destination _____

Airline _____ Flight Number _____

Departure/Arrival _____

Cruise Line/Ship _____ Cabin Number _____

Departure/Arrival _____

Resort/Hotel _____ Phone _____

Reservations _____

PACK THESE ESSENTIALS:

- ☐ Airline tickets
- ☐ Passports/visas
- ☐ Camera, film
- ☐ Sewing kit
- ☐ Medicines/prescriptions
- ☐ Extra contact lenses or glasses
- ☐ Credit cards
- ☐ Toiletries
- ☐ Electrical plug adapters
- ☐ Travel iron
- ☐ Clock radio, travel size
- ☐ Traveler's checks
- ☐ Hair dryer

AFTER-DEATH CHECKLIST

1. Locate important papers.
☐ Death certificate
☐ Insurance policies
☐ Marriage license
☐ Birth certificates
☐ The will
☐ Veteran's discharge papers
☐ Social Security benefits
☐ Most recent tax returns

2. Contact an attorney.

3. File for probate of will.

4. Apply for benefits.
☐ Life insurance proceeds
☐ Retirement plan benefits
☐ Veteran's benefits
☐ Social Security benefits

5. Change titles and ownership.
☐ House
☐ Insurance policies
☐ Automobiles
☐ Your will
☐ Credit cards
☐ Bank accounts
☐ Stocks, bonds, and other investments
☐ Safe-deposit boxes

6. Complete notifications of death.

7. Review finances.

8. File and pay applicable taxes.

FOLLOWING THE DEATH OF A FAMILY MEMBER

1. CONTACT the attorney of the deceased for the location of all the important documents of the deceased's estate.

2. CONTACT your own attorney. If you don't have a good probate attorney, chances are you will need one. The first consultation should be free of charge—if it isn't, something's suspicious.

3. YOU will need to ask for at least ten copies of the death certificate.

4. LOCATE the *original* will and insurance policy. A good place to start is with a known safe-deposit box, etc.

5. LOCATE the deceased's Social Security number. You will need this more than once!

6. THE LETTER of instructions, if one exists, should be located and read thoroughly, to ensure that the specific desires of the deceased are carried out.

7. OBTAIN five copies of your marriage certificate for reasons relating to making claims.

8. IF the deceased had children, then several copies of their birth certificates should be obtained. You won't be able to establish claims for certain Social Security benefits without them.

9. OBTAIN copies of your spouse's certificate of honorable discharge in order to claim any veteran's benefits. Contact the Record Center by phone at: (314) 538-4261 (Army), (314) 538-4141 (Navy, Marines, and Coast Guard), or (314) 538-4243 (Air Force).

10. CONTACT the deceased's employer for details about pension plans and other retirement-plan (stock options, 401 [k] plans) benefits. Get copies of all documents.

11. DETERMINE titles and ownership of all properties (such as home, automobile, boat), and all stocks, bonds, and other investments.

12. FIND OUT whether the deceased's credit accounts, mortgage payments, bank, and utility bills have been kept up-to-date.

13. NOTIFY the deceased's creditors.

life

Events to look forward to

HOLIDAY MEAL COUNTDOWN

Day 7:   • Order whatever meat you plan to serve.

Day 6:   • Choose table linens and decorations.
        • Check supply of dishes and borrow any needed items.
        • Read over recipes and check grocery list.

Day 5:   • Determine seating plan and make name cards.

Day 4:   • Sharpen knives.
        • Shop for fresh produce you plan to fix ahead of schedule.
        • Prepare recipes that can be refrigerated or frozen.

Day 3:   • Complete grocery shopping.
        • Clean house.
        • Bake desserts.

Day 2:   • Pick up meat.
        • Purchase fresh flowers if needed.
        • Set the table.

Day 1:   • Make sure each family member has a job.
        • Stuff your bird and place it in the oven.
        • Do a quick house check.
        • Finish last minute cooking.

GROCERY LIST

Bakery	Frozen Food Section	Misc.
Canned Goods	Fruits	Paper Goods
Dairy	Cleaning Items	Seasonings
Drinks	Meats	Vegetables
Notes:		

TRAVEL PLANNER

CLOTHING

_____ Belts
_____ Blouses
_____ Bras
_____ Coat
_____ Dresses
_____ Gloves
_____ Gowns
_____ Hats
_____ Jackets/raincoat
_____ Jeans
_____ Robe/pajamas
_____ Scarves
_____ Shirts
_____ Shoes
_____ Skirts
_____ Slacks
_____ Slippers
_____ Slips
_____ Socks
_____ Stockings
_____ Suits
_____ Sweaters
_____ Swimsuit
_____ Ties
_____ Underwear

TOILETRIES

_____ Aftershave
_____ Blow dryer
_____ Brush and comb
_____ Creams/lotions
_____ Curling iron
_____ Dental floss
_____ Deodorant
_____ Feminine needs
_____ Hair ornaments
_____ Hairspray
_____ Lipstick
_____ Makeup
_____ Eye makeup
_____ Blusher and brush

_____ Foundation
_____ Powder
_____ Manicure items
_____ Mouthwash
_____ Perfume
_____ Razor
_____ Shampoo, rinse and/or conditioner
_____ Shaving kit
_____ Soap
_____ Sunblock
_____ Talc
_____ Toothbrush/toothpaste

MEDICAL

_____ Adhesive bandages
_____ First-aid ointment
_____ Glasses: extra pair
_____ Insect repellent
_____ Prescription and necessary
_____ Nonprescription medications
_____ Thermometer
_____ Vitamins

MISCELLANEOUS

_____ Address book
_____ Alarm clock
_____ Camera and film
_____ Cash/traveler's checks
_____ Checkbook
_____ Credit cards
_____ Flashlight
_____ Jewelry
_____ Pen
_____ Reading material
_____ Safety pins
_____ Scissors
_____ Sewing kit
_____ Stamps
_____ Sunglasses
_____ Travel tickets
_____ Umbrella (purse-size)

TO DO BEFORE MOVING

One Month Before Moving

☐ Make truck rental reservations or arrangements with a moving company.

☐ Gather moving supplies—boxes, tape, rope.

☐ If moving far away, make any necessary travel arrangements, such as airline, hotel, and rental car reservations. Or plan your travel route if driving.

☐ Save moving receipts—many moving expenses are tax deductible.

☐ Place legal, medical, and insurance records in a safe and accessible place.

☐ Notify the Post Office of your move by using a Change of Address Order form.

☐ Use NOTIFICATION POSTCARDS to notify:
- Family members, businesses, and friends
- Banks, insurance companies, and credit card companies
- Doctors, dentists, and other service providers
- State and federal tax authorities and any other government agencies as needed. (To obtain an IRS change-of-address form, call 1-800-829-3676.)

Two Weeks Before Moving

☐ Inform gas, electric, water, and cable providers of your move. Sign up for services at your new address.

☐ Inform local phone company of your move and choose a long-distance carrier for your new address. Once you have your new phone number, call your long-distance company directly to sign up or transfer special savings programs and services.

☐ Recruit moving-day help.

☐ Confirm travel reservations.

☐ Arrange to close or transfer your bank account, if appropriate.

The Day Before Moving

☐ Set aside moving materials, such as tape measure, pocket knife, rope.

☐ Pick up rental truck.

☐ Check oil and gas in your car.

☐ If traveling, make sure you have tickets, charge cards, and a phone card.

TO DO AFTER MOVING

☐ Mail that has been forwarded from your old address will have a yellow address label on it. Notify the sender of your new address.

☐ Register to vote. Call your local board of elections for specific registration information. Ask them how to notify your previous voting district of your change of address.

☐ If you have moved into a different state, contact the Department of Motor Vehicles to exchange your driver's license.

☐ Call the Department of Sanitation in your new town to find out which day the trash is collected. Also ask about recycling programs.

☐ Call your Chamber of Commerce to get helpful information on:
  • Schools
  • Cable service
  • Cultural events and community activities
  • Libraries and parks
  • Availability of emergency calling services, such as 911

☐ Provide your new doctor and dentist with your medical history. You may have to request your file from your previous doctor/dentist.

☐ Transfer insurance policies to an agent in your new community. You may also wish to make a detailed list of your belongings, their value, and your coverage.

☐ Give your new home a good cleaning.

☐ Scout your new neighborhood for shopping areas. You may need furniture, tools, or housewares unexpectedly.

☐ Seek out new service providers, such as a bank, cleaners, and a veterinarian.

☐ Locate the hospital as well as police and fire stations near your home.

☐ Moving can be stressful. Be sure to monitor the effects of your recent move on your family.

CAMPING CHECKLIST

EQUIPMENT	COOKING UTENSILS
☐ batteries	☐ plates, cups, bowls
☐ flashlights	☐ knives, forks, spoons
☐ fluorescent lanterns	☐ pots, pans, and lids
☐ tent	☐ kettle
☐ tent pegs	☐ cooking forks/spoons
☐ sleeping bags	☐ aluminum foil
☐ foam/air mattress	☐ tongs
☐ ground cover/tarp	☐ pancake turner
☐ rope	☐ knives
☐ canteen	☐ mixing bowls
☐ shovel	☐ plastic containers
☐ hammer	☐ coffeepot
☐ saw	☐ plastic tablecloth
☐ hatchet	☐ camp stove
☐ pocket/sheath knife	☐ can opener
☐ plastic bags	☐ hot pads
☐ garbage sacks	☐ spatula
☐ maps	☐ cooler
☐ compass	☐ charcoal/starter fluid
☐ backpacks	☐ fuel for stove
☐ folding chairs	☐ paper towels
☐ first-aid kit	☐ dish detergent, sponge, scouring pads,
☐ fire extinguisher	towels
☐	☐ dishpan
☐	☐ rubber bands
	☐ masking tape
	☐
	☐

CLOTHES/TOILETRIES

- ☐ leather hiking shoes
- ☐ bathing suits
- ☐ water shoes
- ☐ hats
- ☐ leather belts
- ☐ rain gear
- ☐ jeans/shorts
- ☐ T-shirts
- ☐ long-sleeved shirts
- ☐ jackets/sweatshirts
- ☐ toilet kit—toothbrush, soap, towel, contact case, etc.
- ☐
- ☐

FOOD

- ☐ eggs
- ☐ butter
- ☐ milk
- ☐ water
- ☐ canned food
- ☐ sandwich meats
- ☐ bread
- ☐ cheese
- ☐ pancake/biscuit mix
- ☐ cereal
- ☐ dried fruits/nuts
- ☐ tea/coffee/cocoa
- ☐ marshmallows
- ☐ chocolate bars
- ☐ graham crackers
- ☐
- ☐
- ☐

MISCELLANEOUS

- ☐ binoculars
- ☐ sunglasses
- ☐ camera
- ☐ insect repellent
- ☐ recreational gear
- ☐
- ☐
- ☐
- ☐
- ☐

Business in a Box

Don't work outside the home but would like some extra money? Our greatest idea yet for you . . . a "Business in a Box"! We've found that potpourri sells the best with candy fairly close to it. You can do this any time of day . . . whatever hour you want. It is cash money and is earned instantly! It's not for everyone, but it beats working for someone else at $5 an hour . . . we have easily made $20 to $40 per hour! The plan? Go to any safe neighborhood, knock on the door, and ask if they would be interested in buying a bag of potpourri from you to help with your family expenses. We can count on one hand the times we've been told no. You will find that people think the potpourri or candy bags are cute and most people want to buy—they appreciate your trying to help your family. You can easily make as much money in one day or two than in a week of work somewhere else. Also, you are your own boss and can bag the potpourri while you relax at home watching TV. (Hint: Rich people love the look of the bags for their dinner parties, as do real estate people at open houses.) Some cities do require a peddler's license, so check. Once you do this, you will be shocked at how easy and fast this business is!

Costs

A cardboard box, *silk* ribbon of the ½ inch size, a box of baggies (the fold-over type, generic brand), the $1 bag of potpourri at the $ store (this will make 8 to 10 little baggies), little tags (you can make these from wallpaper books or old cards), a hole puncher, a pair of scissors, 10 one-dollar bills for change. Make your ribbons and tags reflect the holidays as well as just colorful for any occasion. You will also need a basket to carry them in: We sometimes put in a red bandanna in the bottom for the Fourth of July, a paper doily for a more elegant effect, or a swag of Christmas material, plus many more touches. Be creative! But remember, how you look yourself as well as the presentation of your basket will both affect your success.

THIS IS YOUR BOX (FROM "THE AIR" VIEW)

potpourri bag _____	ribbon box (ribbons cut about 10″ long)
potpourri bag	hole puncher and old cards, wallpaper sheets, gift tags, pair of scissors _____
Put another smaller box here to empty your potpourri bags so you can grab a bagful.	grocery-type bag to hold finished baggies
	fold-top baggies

(Customers also love the paper bookmarks!)

Note: I take my Business in a Box when I go to the doctor or have to wait for my children, ball games, etc. You'll be amazed at how many you can make.

P.S. Your profit on the dollar should be about 85 to 90 cents!

Friends,
Hope you have enjoyed our "foolish" and our "serious."

> *thanks for the company!*
> The Tightwad Twins
> Ann and Susan Fox